a
Home for the
Soul

A guide for dwelling
with spirit and imagination

a Home for the Soul

Anthony Lawlor

Photographs by Rick Donhauser

Clarkson Potter/Publishers
New York

Also by Anthony Lawlor

The Temple in the House

Copyright © 1997 by Anthony Lawlor

Illustration credits may be found on page 224.

Published by Clarkson N. Potter/Publishers,
201 East 50th Street, New York, New York 10022.
Member of the Crown Publishing Group.

Random House, Inc. New York, Toronto, London,
Sydney, Auckland

http://www.randomhouse.com

CLARKSON N. POTTER, POTTER, and colophon are trademarks of
Clarkson N. Potter, Inc.

Printed in the United States

Design by 2^b Group, Inc. NY

Library of Congress Cataloging-in-Publication Data
is available upon request.

ISBN 0-517-70400-5

10 9 8 7 6 5 4 3 2 1

First Edition

For Suzanne
and my family

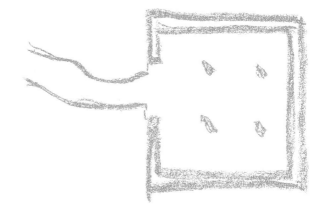

Place is more important than strength.

Vedic proverb

Contents

PART ONE   Chambers of the Soul

PART TWO # Personal Images of the Soul

After practicing architecture for many years, I have learned that any creative work is influenced by numerous people. In this regard, I am indebted to the following friends and colleagues who supported and encouraged this book:

CAROL SOUTHERN, at Clarkson Potter, whose enthusiasm for my work, insightful editing, and understanding of the connection between soul and architecture were invaluable in clarifying and refining the direction of the book;

ROBBIN GOURLEY, at Clarkson Potter, and BOB STERN and BARBARA GRZESLO, of the 2^b Group, whose keen design sense rendered the words and images into a beautiful book;

RICK DONHAUSER, whose collaboration in translating the written concepts into photographic form added vitality to the material;

MURIEL NELLIS, my literary agent, whose brilliance, heart, and integrity give practical sustenance to my work;

SUZANNE LAWLOR, my wife, whose dedication to inviting soul into our home provided much of the insight and inspiration for this book;

SUE WELLER, my design partner, whose creativity over the years has helped me understand how architecture can nourish the soul;

MY CLIENTS, whose desire to make homes for the soul has shown me the pathways of shaping matter with spirit;

and the families and individuals who allowed their homes to be photographed for this book.

I

The Journey Homeward

FROM THE MOMENT WE ARE BORN, WE SEEM COMPELLED

TO TRAVEL HOMEWARD. IN PLACES AND PEOPLE, WE SEEK

THAT ELUSIVE FEELING OF BEING WELCOMED. HOME IS

THE GOAL OF THE EPIC JOURNEYS OF THE HUMAN SPIRIT.

JESUS RETURNS TO HIS HEAVENLY FATHER. MOSES LEADS

HIS PEOPLE TO THEIR HOMELAND. BUDDHA REACHES THE

IMMOVABLE SPOT OF ENLIGHTENMENT BENEATH THE BO

TREE. THE ADVENTURES AND TRIALS OF THE *Odyssey*

ARRIVE AT THE FOLLOWING SCENE:

> *Then the well-ordered hall was filled with rejoicing. The minstrel drew sweet sounds from his lyre and waked in all the longing for dance. Gaily they trod a measure, men and fair-robed women, till the great house rang with their footfalls. For Odysseus at last after long wandering had come home and every heart was glad.*

Despite this primal craving for home, our dwelling places often fail to receive us with care and artfulness. We want our houses and apartments to be warm, nurturing, and beautiful, but they are sometimes areas of chaos and territories of conflict, isolation, and confusion. The very places that hold the promise of harmony and revitalization can, instead, be the abodes of disorder, friction, and loneliness.

The tumult of modern life that surrounds our homes doesn't help the situation. Crime, violence, job insecurity, environmental pollution, and a litany of other problems rumble outside our doors. The hectic pace of work and community life can leave us stressed out and exhausted.

Yet, as Meister Eckehart writes, "God is at home, it is we who have gone out for a walk." The haven that the soul seeks is close at hand, within the stove and the cupboard, on the bookshelf, and in the closet. With the eyes to see it and the hands to create it, we can recover the home that the soul desires.

To help you perceive and create a home for the soul is the purpose of this book. It is a signpost for assisting the soul on its homeward journey. The following pages invite you to discover the abode of inspiration and delight that is hidden within your house or apartment, the one that goes unnoticed in the hectic pace of modern life. The book discusses how each room in your home can care for a different aspect of your soul and how all the rooms together can renew and enliven wholeness within you. Based on these insights, the book also provides suggestions for establishing a soulful dwelling place through rearranging your existing home or apartment, renovating it, or building a new house.

A Home for the Soul is not another self-improvement program to add to your already busy schedule. It is, instead, about shifting attention from the outer surfaces of walls and furniture to their inner depths. It is also about acting in ways within your available time and budget that can transform your living environment into a home that nurtures the soul. Reading this book will help you reconnect the form and function of your physical surroundings to the elusive shape of the human spirit. Remodeling our consciousness, we can see the deeper workings of the spirit and rearrange our furnishings, and maybe our walls, to support the vitality of the soul.

Each room and piece of furniture can be used to deepen the experience of soulfulness. The material in this book investigates ways that your innermost needs and dreams shape your surroundings and how those surroundings might be enhanced to serve the core of your being.

Home offers a practical setting for fostering soul in concrete ways. It serves the requirements of shelter and food while simultaneously addressing our deeper needs for love, wisdom, and establishing a place in the world. The bedroom, bathroom, kitchen, and other rooms are indispensable to the basic functions of sleeping, bathing, eating, and gathering. They are also places where the soul can receive the bed's restfulness, the bath's invigoration, and the stove's nourishment.

Living within the sprawl of modern cities, it is easy to feel that we dwell in an isolated, fragmented wasteland. A dry, alienating environment can be transformed when we understand how houses and apartments can care for the soul. By linking ourselves to places and circumstances, we can deepen a felt connection to our home and learn specific means of nourishing the soul.

Most of us have never learned the fundamental knowledge of how the rooms we inhabit can serve the needs of the spirit. Modern design focuses on the sterile objects of form and function. A house is defined by the statistics of cost, square footage, and style. It is all too seldom that a real estate agent asks, "What is the feeling you are looking for in a house or apartment?" An architect may ask about your requirements for kitchen appliances, closet space, and other physical necessities, but he or she will seldom inquire about the qualities of soul you would like expressed in the design.

If we do not learn how our homes can care for the soul, there will always be a gap between who we are and where we live. We will inevitably create dwellings of loneliness and alienation. The intention of this book is to offer a means of restoring the connection between ourselves and our surroundings and provide ways of weaving spirit into the places we inhabit. This book invites you to rediscover the spiritual dimensions that give form to every room of your home, but go unnoticed.

The soul's path is a journey toward home.

Modern modes of dwelling do not reach these depths of experience. Our materialistic worldview neglects the revitalizing powers of the soul. Surrounded by technological comforts, many of us long for a way of life that encourages enrichment and meaning. We search for inspiration and a sense of sacredness that is natural, practical, personal, and immediate.

In working with Rick Donhauser to create the photographs for this book, we attempted to take a fresh approach. We wanted to avoid the standard catalog of unusual locations and design ideas provided by most books and magazines on the subject. Instead we looked deeply into our immediate surroundings, a small Midwestern town, and gleaned vignettes that would portray a symbolic home for the soul. The intention of these images is to encourage you to look more closely at your own surroundings and discover, firsthand, the forms, textures, and colors that embody the workings of soul.

The premise of this book is that the sacredness we seek can be found right under our noses, in the environments we inhabit. It reflects the idea written by the Lakota medicine man Lame Deer in his book Lame Deer, Seeker of Visions:

What do you see here, my friend? Just an ordinary old cooking pot, black with soot and full of dents. It is standing on the fire on top of that old woodstove, and the water bubbles and moves the lid as the white steam rises to the ceiling. It doesn't seem to have a message, that old pot, and I guess you don't give it a thought. [But] I think about ordinary, common things like this pot. The bubbling water comes from the rain cloud. It represents the sky. The fire comes from the sun, which warms us all. The steam is living breath. It was water; now it goes up to the sky, becomes a cloud again. We Sioux spend a lot of time thinking about everyday things, which in our mind

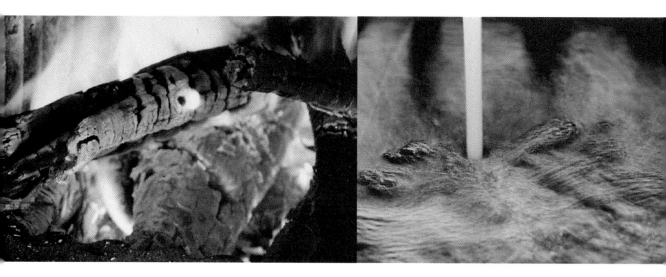

are mixed up with the spiritual. We see in the world around us many symbols that teach us the meaning of life. We try to understand them not with the head but with the heart, and we need no more than a hint to give us the meaning.

To this end, the following pages present a new way of seeing, one that translates common spaces and objects into symbols of the inner workings of the spirit. Daily life is filled with items of symbolic importance. The flag, the cross, the dollar sign, and other common emblems concentrate myriad levels of meaning into simple forms. Yet, the psychological power contained in ordinary places such as kitchens, gathering rooms, and bedrooms is often overlooked. By gaining an understanding of the symbolic content of rooms and furnishings, we can be nourished by the inner radiance of the soul— the life force that is hidden by the solid, outward appearance of matter. Discovering the links between spirit and form, we are better able to create homes that express our true nature in daily life.

Symbols are windows onto the unseen forces that shape us. They are points of breakthrough where vital sparks of energy and imagination can burst into mundane existence. We use a wedding ring, for example, to symbolize the invisible bonds of love that unify two people. When we learn to see such common objects as stoves and bathtubs as symbols of nourishment and transformation, the rigid boundaries that trap our hearts and minds can become transparent to the workings of the spirit.

To ignore the vitality hidden within the symbols that surround us is to cut ourselves off from the healing and renewing powers of the soul. The following pages offer ways of removing the lenses that cloud our vision and noticing how intimate spaces and small things can serve to establish soulful dwelling places.

This symbolic view of home provides a glimpse of broader and deeper possibilities of living. It kindles imagination and creativity. It allows you to find harmonious relationships within the seemingly opposing forces in your surroundings. Mundane modes of living can then become richer and more stimulating. By seeing our homes as symbols of the unseen patterns of the spirit, daily life can become permeated with purpose and significance.

Through my writing and your reading we can re-envision your house or apartment as a sacred setting where depth and meaning are a concrete reality. Each room and activity can become a means of delighting the soul. The journey homeward can find its goal in a place that invites you to bring forth who you truly are and what you want to become.

2

The Vessel of Soulmaking

HOME IS A CONTAINER OF SOUL. THE ROOF AND WALLS SHELTER AND NURTURE THE SPARK OF LIFE THAT ANIMATES OUR MODES OF DWELLING. THEY DEFINE THE SETTING WHERE SOUL IS TRANSFORMED FROM RAW ENERGY INTO THE MYRIAD EXPERIENCES OF LIVING. FURNITURE, CLOTHING, AND OTHER OBJECTS FOSTER THE INNER WORK OF THE PSYCHE. A STOVE, FOR EXAMPLE, IS AN APPLIANCE THAT TRANSLATES THE UNDEFINED STUFF OF SPIRIT INTO EXPERIENCES OF NOURISHMENT. THE BED ENCOURAGES THE SOUL TO DREAM AND MAKE LOVE. EACH ELEMENT OF A HOME PLAYS ITS ROLE IN BRINGING FORTH THE LATENT POSSIBILITIES OF SOUL.

Theories about soul can make it seem dry and abstract, but the walls and furnishings of a home allow us to care for the psyche directly and immediately. The grainy touch and subtle hues of an oak table, for example, can nourish the soul's desire for richness and connection with nature. Water gurgling in the bathtub, sunlight sparkling on a windowsill, flowers scenting the air, and numerous other experiences invite soul to enter the rooms of our houses and apartments.

The headlines of spiritual experience are often grabbed by dramatic tales of angelic light and celestial encounters, but soulfulness mainly grows within the realms of everyday life. A cozy moment in bed that warms a deep place within us, a conversation at the kitchen table that connects parent and child, and other common experiences sustain and enrich the depths of who we are.

The needs of soul are satisfied through the archetypal actions of human dwelling—cooking, eating, gathering with others, sleeping, dreaming, lovemaking, bathing, managing finances, and solitude. Cooking, for example, is a practical activity that creates edible meals; it also cares for the soul's creative urge to transform the raw stuff of life into digestible and appetizing forms. Eating satisfies the hunger in our bellies, but it also satisfies the soul's desire for fulfillment. Each room in a home is a physical setting that supports a different archetypal action. Taken together, the rooms of a home encompass the full circle of the soul. They serve as a microcosm for understanding and working with the totality of mind and body.

The rooms and furniture of your home are more than a mere collection of isolated objects. They are tangible nurturers of soul. In discussing how houses and apartments can care for and delight the soul, I would like to clarify what I mean by soul and a home that can contain it.

SOUL

Soul is the force that animates our thoughts, words, and actions. Soul is also the wisdom that gives specific form to this animating force. Plato wrote in his *Laws:* "Soul is among the primal things, elder-born than all the bodies and prime source of all their changes and transformations." Being the source that gives rise to form, soul cannot be precisely defined by specific words or architectural forms. Written phrases or physical shapes can merely conjure up images that point toward soul's subtle movements and elusive nature. The terms commonly used to describe soul are *God, life force, consciousness, psyche, Self,* and *inner nature.*

Soul can be imagined as an ocean of water. The ocean is primordial and inexhaustible, the source of life, the realm of pure potential and infinite possibilities. At the depths of the ocean the water is silent and still, unfathomable and mysterious. The surface of the ocean rises into an innumerable assortment of waves: large and small, fast and slow, rolling and crashing. In some places the ocean becomes solid ice. In others, it turns into airy vapor, ascending to become clouds and rain.

Soul takes on similar qualities within us. At the depths of our being, soul is quiet, profound, and boundless. On the surface, soul flows into the countless variety of emotions and thoughts that propel our actions. Sometimes, soul is experienced as gentle softness; at other times, it has a firm power.

Despite its elusive nature, soul has specific qualities we intuitively understand. Genuineness, depth, and connectedness are qualities that characterize soulful experience. In *Care of the Soul*, Thomas Moore writes that "soulfulness is tied to the particulars of life—good food, satisfying conversation, genuine friends, and experiences that touch the heart." Soul is nourished by variety, quirks, and idiosyncrasies.

Soul is the glue that links mind to body, body to home, home to earth, and earth to cosmos. It yokes the rooms in a home to the events that take place within them. Through these connections soul ties together the memories that describe our personal history. "We see the world piece by piece," wrote Emerson, "as the sun, the moon, the animal, the tree: but the whole, of which these are the shining parts, is the soul."

Soul is not necessarily linked to religion. Someone may access soul through the prayers, rituals, and scriptures of their faith; but they can also encounter soul in a flavorful stew, the caress of a lover, or the textures of a pine floor. A chapel within a vast cathedral may be a shrine of spiritual peace, but a window seat within a living room can offer a haven of quiet renewal.

Soul is the spiritual well from which our thoughts and actions pour, yet it is beyond our ability to create and control. We can stand at the rim of this well and peer into the waters of the soul, but we can never fully perceive its depths. Underground springs and unseen currents move within the soul; we see only the ripples and splashes on its surface. "The mystery," writes Phil Cousineau in *Soul: An Archaeology*, "[is how soul] ignites the spark of life where there was none before and carves out a cavernous inner dimension unique to all things. . . . The mystery of soul is its paradox of unchanging depths in an ever-changing universe."

A HOME FOR THE SOUL

Since the soul is vast and unfathomable, the characteristics of a home that attends to its needs cannot be captured in a simple laundry list of attributes. Certain qualities, however, can point us in the direction of experiencing greater depth and meaning within our houses and apartments.

A home for the soul inspires our dreams.

A home for the soul sparks our imagination. Its architecture and furnishings offer more than mechanical function and urge us to explore the essence of who we truly are. Colors, textures, and shapes act as bridges that lead our attention from the material world of isolated objects into the interconnected realm of the spirit. A home for the soul offers more than one level of experience at a time. It simultaneously addresses all levels of mind, body, and environment—our myths, emotions, thoughts, senses, actions, bodily functions, and the ecological processes of nature. The bathtub of such a home might honor Venus's desire for beauty, ease the conflict of a hectic day, warm and soothe the body, cleanse the skin's pores, and connect us to the sprinkling of rain and the flowing of streams.

A home for the soul is not a material goal to be acquired, but a setting for inquiring into the processes of living. Within its walls we can discover how the

A pumpkin and dried corn by an entry honor a change of season.

25

germ of consciousness within us grows to become the events and circumstances that define our existence. We can discern the links between our personal needs and dreams and the universal forces that shape the cosmos. In a home for the soul, common objects and actions become symbols that at once hide and reveal the deeper powers that animate our lives.

A home for the soul has character and personality. It contains rich textures and colors that invite the hand and delight the eye. It reflects subtle gradations of light that range from murky shadows to shimmering points of illumination. Forms are imaginative and reveal how they support activity. There is care and attention to detail. Natural materials such as wood, stone, wool, silk, and cotton are used to create an environment that opens to the vitality of sunlight and fresh air. A home for the soul is a sensuous dwelling place that urges us to savor the mingling of spirit and matter.

The details of such a home are interconnected with the wholeness of the soul. Rooms and furnishings gain order and harmony by reflecting the organizing principles of nature. Design elements reflect the proportions and scale of the human body. Windows and doorways acknowledge the path of the sun and moon. There is a connection to local landforms, plants, animals, and weather patterns.

The traditional homes of Europe call to mind one example of the classic look and feel of a home for the soul. Thatched or tiled roofs, plaster walls, and oak doors offer the soul dwelling places of stability, feeling, and creativity. Sunlight shining through the windows glances off the thick walls in subtle nuances of shade and shadow. Cast-iron stoves, stone fireplaces, dormer windows, and other details please the soul and invite it to stay.

Despite our attraction to homes with these qualities, most of the houses and apartments built in America since the early part of this century have left soul out in the cold. In the rush to create cheap, efficient, and hygienic housing, many architects and builders have neglected the deeper needs and dreams of our hearts and minds. The featureless Sheetrock walls and ceilings of shoebox apartments and faceless ranch houses provide impersonal containers for our possessions. They do little to create vessels for soulmaking. Until recently, twentieth-century kitchens tended to look more like laboratories for the dissection of plants and animals than places for engaging in the spiritual alchemy of soul work.

Cheap, efficient housing can leave soul out in the cold.

Yet, recent approaches to design are inviting the soul to return home from its exile. Kitchens with the earthy textures of pine cabinets, granite countertops, and substantial stoves are calling soul to the family hearth. Bathrooms with soaking tubs, floral tonics, and herbal body oils create havens for soothing mind and body. Even hard-edged designs that employ weathered steel, sandblasted glass, or concrete block create dwelling places with a graininess and depth that are more attractive to soul than the sterile homes of the 1950s and 1960s.

A home for the soul, however, is not the result of a particular style of design. A rose-covered cottage in the country

The Hauptman Residence, Fairfield, Iowa, uses reinterpretations of soulful traditional elements in this wraparound porch.

might seem like an obvious candidate for "soul style," but depth and richness can be created using forms as diverse as a Victorian row house, a Santa Fe hacienda, or a loft in a converted industrial building.

Repeating the past is not a necessary part of creating dwelling places of the soul. The house called Fallingwater designed by Frank

Lloyd Wright is a masterpiece of modern design. Its angular geometries, daring structural shape, and imaginative combination of stone, stucco, and glass create a home that expands the possibilities of soulful dwelling. Even minimalist or deconstructivist designs, such as those by Frank Gehry, can care for the soul if natural materials, rich colors, and sensuous forms are crafted to inspire the mind and delight the body.

An expensive house or apartment is not required to care for the soul. Simple objects and furnishings can become touchstones of inspiration and meaning. A plain bookshelf, holding photographs of family and friends or a collection of personal mementos, creates a haven that nurtures the soul. Taking a bath by candlelight can transform an act of functional hygiene into an experience that renews the spirit.

CREATING A HOME FOR THE SOUL

A home for the soul is created by making soul the reference point for the forms, textures, materials, and colors of a house or apartment. Most approaches to design focus on the style and functionality of objects. A home for the soul honors the hearts and minds of the people who use those objects. I once heard the architect Michael Graves reflect on this idea by describing a chair he designed as being more like the people who used the chair than the machine that made it. In other words, a home for the soul is composed of doorways, sofas, and other elements that support and nurture the core being of the people who live there. A desk, for instance, would not be selected because it was a Craftsman style and harmonized with other furniture in the room. It would be chosen for the ways its color, texture, and shape inspired soul.

The Bloedel Residence, Bainbridge Island, Washington, by James Cutler Architects, creates a soulful setting. The house was built as a memorial to Prentice Bloedel's wife of sixty-two years: a place to remember her with a view toward her unmarked grave site.

An entire home could be arranged according to this approach. The floor of each room could have materials and patterns that support the soul. The walls might be painted with colors that embrace the soul. The ceiling could be lighted to uplift the soul. Furniture, cabinets, and appliances could be selected to honor the activities of the soul.

MATERIALS

The textures and subtle hues of clay roofing tiles evoke the image of soulful shelter.

Building and decorating materials have a powerful effect on the soulfulness of a home. Materials found in nature or those created with a minimum of technology tend to delight the soul more than high-tech products. A wood or stone countertop enriches the soul more than one made of plastic laminate. A wool rug invites the soul more than a carpet made of acrylic fibers.

Besides their richness of texture and appearance, natural materials also contain mythic and symbolic qualities. Vedic philosophy, for example, considers wood the primal material of the universe. The Taittiriya Brahmana states that "Brahman [the Primordial Totality] was the wood, Brahman was the tree from which they shaped heaven and earth." In numerous cultures, wooden objects are associated with rites of passage—cradles at birth and coffins at death, marriage beds, and gallows crosses. Many Christians see Christ as the cosmic carpenter who fashions the house of divine life out of the wood of the universe.

Each species of wood expresses a different character of soul through its particular hardness, texture, color, resistance to decay, and usefulness. Oak, for example, is a strong hardwood that expresses protection, courage, and durability. Because the Romans thought that oak trees attracted lightning, they linked oak with the thunderbolts of the sky god, Jupiter, and his wife, Juno, the goddess of marriage. Each year the wedding of Jupiter and Juno was celebrated by devotees wearing crowns of oak leaves in a grove of oak trees, making the oak a symbol of conjugal fidelity and fulfillment. For Christians, oak expresses strength in adversity, since oak is said to be the tree of the Cross. Druid oracles prepared themselves to make prophecies by eating acorns.

Cedar, which resists decay, embodies indestructibility. It was the Cosmic Tree of Life for the ancient Sumerians. Cedar is considered by the Jews to be the wood of Solomon's Temple. An early Christian writer, Origen, noted that "cedar does not decay. To use cedar in the beams of a house is to protect our soul from corruption."

Pine, the product of evergreen trees, is a symbol of directness, masculinity, and immortality. Europeans believed that pine preserved the body from decay.

Birch signifies fertility and light. In Europe, birch wood was thought to drive out evil spirits and provide protection from witches. Criminals and the mentally ill were beaten with birch switches. Shamans in Europe considered birch the Cosmic Tree, which their spirits ascended through seven stages to the Supreme Spirit. Nordic mythology prophesies that the final world battle will take place around a birch tree.

Sand-cast brick, made by combining earth, water, and fire, provides depth and richness.

Ash is the emblem of adaptability, prudence, and modesty. The Greeks called the nymphs of ash trees Meliae, who were born from the drops of blood that fell when Zeus castrated his father, Cronus. In Scandinavia, ash is the Yggdrasil, the cosmic tree, the source of life and immortality, which united the three worlds of the abyss, earth, and heaven with roots that reached into the underworld, a trunk that passed through human life, and branches that stretched to heaven. The gods were said to gather beneath the branches of an ash.

Stone, on the other hand, expresses the soul qualities of stability and durability. It is a symbol of the eternal and the indestructible. The timeless character of stone reflects the processes that created it. Granite, marble, and other stones were the first materials of a newly formed planet hundreds of millions of years ago. Deep within the bowels of the earth underground rivers of molten rock slowly cooled

Weathered oak siding expresses the changing qualities of the spirit.

Coursed stone blocks reflect the soul's timeless nature.

and crystallized, rising to the earth's crust as stone. Shifts in the earth's crust heaved the stone to the surface as mountains and deposits of rock.

Despite its solid appearance, ancient people saw sacred forces dwelling within stone. It produced the sparks that ignited the fire of the family hearth. Certain stones were thought to contain powers of healing and increased fertility. A Greek legend describes a new human race that was born from stones after a cataclysmic flood. In the ancient

Painted wood against stained cedar reflects a spectrum of soulful textures.

Irish city of Tara, a "stone of knowledge" called Fal was said to cry out when it was touched by the rightful king.

In buildings, the ceremony of laying the cornerstone marks the symbolic birth of the building. The keystone at the zenith of a stone arch stabilizes the structure, allowing dense matter to gracefully span habitable space. In Freemasonry, the "rough stone" stands for the apprentice who aspires to become a "hewn stone" who can provide wise and compassionate service in the "temple" of humanity. The transformation of stone from rough to hewn was used as a metaphor for the transformation of one's consciousness from ignorance to enlightenment.

Man-made products that combine natural materials also embody primal elements. Brick and ceramic tile are produced by blending earth, water, and fire. Glass is created from fire and sand; wool from animal fleece; cotton from growing plants. Within a home constructed and furnished with materials from nature, the soul can feel connected to the substances and processes that create the world.

DWELLING WITH SOUL

The primary ingredient in creating a home for the soul is our conscious attention. By bringing care and positive regard to the daily actions of living, we can deepen and foster soulfulness in ourselves and our surroundings.

The approach I discuss in this book differs from those spiritual attitudes that disconnect the soul from the body and environment. It also differs from the materialistic view of modern life that separates spirit from matter, and mind from body. These perspectives see the material world as a prison that traps the freedom of the soul. They make happiness and meaning seem attainable only by escaping the bonds of the world. Since having a body and dwelling in the material world are part and parcel of being human, these attitudes put off sacred experience until those times when one transcends daily existence or ascends to a heavenly realm.

The home for the soul discussed in these pages, in contrast, is attained within the walls that contain human life.

Greene and Greene combined redwood shingles, oak trim, and leaded glass at the Thorsen House to create a home that is at once elegant and earthy.

This home urges us to find sacredness in the here and now of daily living. Cooking, eating, bathing, and the other specific actions of dwelling become a means for reconnecting mind, body, environment, and spirit to the integrated wholeness of the psyche. Within such a home, each distinct action can be experienced as a step in the cycle of creating, dissolving, and re-creating life. Simple tasks can become pathways to deepening soulfulness in daily life.

Hammered metal and stained redwood are used in this Berkeley house to honor the arrival of mail.

3

Caring for Home,
Fostering Soul

THE MOST IMMEDIATE WAY OF DEEPENING SOULFULNESS IN A HOME IS THROUGH CLEANING AND REPAIR. HOUSEWORK, HOWEVER, IS DENIGRATED IN OUR SOCIETY, AND WE USUALLY OVERLOOK THE POWER OF PURIFICATION AND MAINTENANCE IN FOSTERING SOUL. THE INTENT OF MOST SPIRITUAL PRACTICES, IN FACT, IS THE TRANSFORMATION OF DISORDER INTO ORDER. MEDITATION, FOR EXAMPLE, ALLOWS THE MIND TO TRANSCEND RANDOM EXCITATIONS OF THINKING AND GAIN MENTAL COHERENCE AND PEACE. YOGA UNWINDS THE TANGLE OF STRESS IN THE BODY AND BALANCES THE FLOW OF ENERGY THROUGH IT. COMPASSIONATE ACTION IS INTENDED TO TRANSFORM FRICTION INTO HARMONY.

The word *cleaning* conveys this spiritual connotation. The roots of the word *clean* suggest the purity conferred by a ceremonial anointing with oil. Cleaning in this sense bestows a blessing on a house or apartment. It makes whole the life of the house.

Another essential component of spiritual practice is discernment, separating those things that honor the soul from those that do not.

Cleaning is the act of discerning what will benefit our homes and removing what will not. Accumulating unnecessary and unused objects is a negative side effect in a consumer society. Most of us have closets and shelves filled with clothing, books, electronic gadgets, and other goods that we haven't used in years. Cleaning allows us to discern those objects that enhance the flow of soul in a home from those that stifle that flow. It can provide an avenue for passing on unused items to those who could gain pleasure from them.

An Indian woman washes the steps of a ghat by the Ganges, a practical act of purification and renewal.

Cleaning requires that we slow down and spend more time being attentive to our surroundings, which is another technique for opening to spiritual experience. One of the central tenets of Zen practice, for instance, is to eat while you eat and walk while you walk. In other words, let go of the constant mental chatter of regretting the past and fearing the future, focusing mind and body on the vivid reality of the present moment. Traditionally, this "centered" state of mind/body integration was achieved through such tasks as attentively raking the gravel of a Zen garden in precise pat-

Sponging, scrubbing, and sweeping allow us to slow down, be more attentive to our surroundings, and enliven soulfulness in our homes.

terns or washing a tea bowl with care. In the rush of modern living, cleaning can be a technique for settling down and engaging in the simple pleasures of bringing order to our personal corner of the world. Through cleaning we can experience our power to effect simple change and accomplish immediate results.

One of the central afflictions in contemporary society is the feeling of being out of touch and isolated from our surroundings. Caring for our homes is a practical way of establishing a felt connection to our dwelling places. The touch of the hand links spirit to surroundings through washing, polishing, and rearranging. Through such conscious actions, the cleaning touch can become a means of healing the relationship of spirit and matter. Homemaking then becomes a pathway for soulmaking.

Cleaning does not imply the compulsive work of creating a sterile environment. It is the artful care of objects that supports the needs and dreams of the soul, as this story about the Japanese tea master Sen no Rikyu implies. One day Rikyu asked his son Do-an to clean the path leading through the tea garden. Do-an swept and scrubbed each stepping-stone with the greatest of care and then asked his father to inspect the work. "Not complete" was the master's response. Do-an repeated the task with even greater mindfulness until each speck of dust and pine needle was washed away. He called his father a second time to look over his work, and again it was not accepted. After a third cleaning, Do-an was certain that the path was in perfect condition, but Rikyu just shook his head. In desperation the son threw up his hands and shouted, "Well, you show me how to do it, then!" The tea master walked to a small maple tree near the path, grabbed the trunk, and gave it a vigorous shake. A rain of autumn leaves sprinkled the path with an array of dazzling colors. "Now the garden is perfect," he said.

Repairing worn or broken objects is also essential to creating a home for the soul. In our rush to discard the old and bring in the new, we can lose touch with the history we share with furnishings, clothes,

A common broom can become an implement for fostering soul in a home.

and other things. Dents, scratches, and rips hold the memory of our interaction with the environment. My wife tells the story of her mother's samovar that was lassoed by her brother as a young cowboy. The resulting dent became a reference point for that chapter of family lore. In our own household, a French porcelain bowl, received as a wedding present, has been broken and mended several times. The original beauty of the bowl has gained a unique character that is intimately connected to the soul of our home.

Repairing such defects revives the usefulness of worn objects and gives them a richness and depth that cannot be found in new articles. An antique is nothing other than an old piece of furniture that has been cared for and mended for many years. When antiques are too costly or not available, architecture and furnishings are often made to appear old to increase their sense of soulfulness. New houses are built with the ruddy texture of sand-cast bricks. Hardwood floors and furniture are "distressed"—charred and scrubbed with a wire brush—for a timeworn look. Paint is dabbed on with sponges to replicate the venerable plaster walls of Tuscan villas.

The word *repair* also means to return home. Cleaning blesses our houses and apartments with care, and mending readies our dwelling places for the soul's return home. The following chapters describe how each room in your home can be perceived and designed to nourish a different aspect of the soul. Together, the rooms of your home can support the complete spectrum of your spirit's needs and dreams.

PART ONE

Chambers of the Soul

4

Kitchens

THE KITCHEN IS THE CORE OF HOME. DEEP WITHIN OUR BONES IS THE ANCESTRAL MEMORY OF GATHERING ABOUT THE ANCIENT FIRE FOR WARMTH, FOOD, FRIEND-SHIP, AND REGAINING A FELT CONNECTION TO THE SOUL. THE KITCHEN OF A HOME FOR THE SOUL COMBINES THE ELEMENTAL FORCES OF FIRE, WATER, AND EARTH INTO A SETTING THAT ALLOWS US TO RECONNECT WITH THE ELUSIVE ENERGIES THAT IGNITE, NURTURE, AND TRANS-FORM LIFE.

The Greeks understood the mystery of fire when they perceived Hestia, the goddess of the hearth, as the most essential yet mysterious of the gods. They believed that no statue with human or animal features could embody her fiery nature. In her temple, Hestia was honored instead by a sacred fire. Hestia's temple was round and covered by a dome, providing a clear architectural image of the hearth goddess's character. The circular forms ringing the central fire conveyed the idea that fire, like the soul, is a formless essence that we gather around. Returning to the flame of the kitchen, we can be renewed by the miracle of creation, the processes through which warmth and creative energy establish and maintain a home.

Psychologist Barbara Kirksey points out that the loss of connection to the central flame can make us feel "off-center," "off-base," "unsettled," "spaced out," and "off the wall." "Without Hestia," she writes, "there are no boundaries that differentiate the intimacy of the inner dwelling and the outer world, for there is no psychic house to give protective walls. There can be no joyous feast, no celebrations of life, no food for the soul."

Placing the kitchen's fire at the psychological center of a home honors it as a primal source of balanced nourishment. It recalls Hestia's role in maintaining the health of society. The Roman temples that honored Vesta, Hestia's Roman counterpart, were tended by the well-known priestesses called the vestal virgins. Each priestess took a vow of chastity that was thought to strengthen her ability to communicate with the gods, thereby nourishing society with sacred insight and wisdom.

The heat and light of fire make the kitchen a focal point of dwelling.

This stable central fire has always been the focal point of home. Ovid writes that *focus* is the Latin word for hearth and that "the hearth (*focus*) is so named from the flames, and because it fosters all things." The worldly activities of work and school as well as the home activities of cooking and gathering are so many rays of consciousness that gain their focus in relation to the flames of the hearth.

Fire can play this central role because it directly expresses the powers of the soul. "The Lord thy God is a consuming fire," declares the Bible. In the Bhagavad Gita, Lord Krishna states, "I am the fire residing in the bodies of all things that have life." When Prometheus filched fire from the gods and brought it to earth, he made it possible for humans to cook food and gain warmth, allowing us to transform raw foodstuffs into edible meals. Fire's purifying qualities purge dishes and utensils of harmful bacteria with heated water.

THE STOVE

The stove houses Hestia's feminine, transmuting power, recalling the womb and the place of birth. Mircea Eliade writes in *The Forge and the Crucible* that "according to the myths of certain primitive peoples, the aged women of the tribe 'naturally' possessed fire in their genital organs and made use of it to do their cooking" and "that fire, being produced by the friction of two pieces of wood (that is, by their sexual union), was regarded as existing naturally within the piece that represented the female."

The fairy tale of the goose maid uses a stove as the setting for the transformation of consciousness. It seems that an old king's daughter traveled to a far-off kingdom to be married. During the journey, the maid-in-waiting stole the princess's horse and donned her royal garments. The servant told the princess that she would die if she revealed her regal birthright. The princess wandered through the kingdom until a kindly couple took her in and gave her work tending their flock of geese.

After a time the old king came looking for his daughter. He did not recognize her, however, in the guise of a goose girl who cried all day as she tended her flock. The old king asked the goose girl who she was and why she was so sad. The girl replied that telling him would cause her death. The old king took the girl to a nearby house and suggested that she tell her sorrows to the stove. The girl crept into the stove to unburden her heart. She said, "Here I am deserted by the whole world, but I am the old king's daughter. A cruel servant forced me to take off my royal clothes. This servant has taken my place with my bridegroom, and I have to perform menial service as a goose girl. If this my mother knew, her heart would break in two."

Fire makes the kitchen the nourishing and transforming center of home.

The old king stood outside and listened through the stovepipe. When he heard his daughter's plight, he brought her into her rightful place as the bride and queen beside the new king.

In the tale of Hansel and Gretel, the stove becomes a means of

burning away obstacles that repress the soul's vitality. The old witch locks Hansel in a cage, fattening him up to be cooked and devoured. Instead, the witch is pushed into the flames by the young sister. When the children are free, Hansel "springs like a bird"—an archetypal symbol for the soul—from his cage.

The design of modern stoves also displays the shape of archetypal forces. The radial spokes of the burners found on most stoves recall the rays of the sun. The circular dials controlling temperature also reflect this solar theme. Transformations of the food placed on the burners or in the oven occur during the beat of time, in minutes and hours, and most stoves are equipped with timers that regulate cooking. The dark interior of the oven is a cave of mystery where prepared food is inserted and then removed, transfigured into edible, nourishing form.

Thick prongs on a commercial-strength stove recall solar cycles of change.

The flames of the hearth have ancient associations with ashes. In fairy tales, ashes are a sign of engaging the depths of soul work. They indicate the grounding of the psyche that may be unbalanced, isolated, or numb. Characters such as Cinderella (Cinder Girl) or the Norwegian Askaladden (Ash Boy) work in the kitchen, passing from immature, unconscious modes of being into stronger, truer experiences of self-understanding. As Robert Bly points out in *Iron John*: "Ashes, we note, find their way into the whorls of our fingertips, cling there, make the whorls more noticeable, more visible, more clear to us. We can take our own fingerprints with ashes."

Ashes contain the concentrated power of what was burned. They remind us of life's impermanence and a return to the primordial state: "Ashes to ashes, dust to dust." Ashes signify humility. They enrich the soil of consciousness with the hope for new life by showing us that life, like the mythic phoenix, cannot be destroyed, only transformed into a new form.

THE SINK

Fire needs water to do its kitchen work. Cooking is largely a matter of heating the water within foods (such as stir-frying vegetables) or heat-

ing foods that are placed in hot water (such as boiling pasta and simmering soups). Combining fire and water brings together the two great
principles of the soul: creative and receptive, active and passive, yang
and yin, Father Sky and Mother Earth. In their gross forms, fire and
water are in conflict; they struggle to cancel each other out. Water
douses fire. Fire dissolves water into vapor. At a deeper level, fire and
water become heat and moisture, cooperating to create and sustain life.

A two-pronged, swiveling towel holder adds
layers of detail to this sink cabinet. Fabric
hung below a kitchen sink softens and
warms the otherwise hard and cool effect
of all-wood or plastic-laminate cabinets.

Flowing water purifies food
in preparation for cooking.

Water makes fire useful. Flames burn food that is not tempered by
water. Kohler, a manufacturer of plumbing fixtures, borrowed an
image from Indian mythology in naming one of its new kitchen
faucets the Avatar. In Vedic philosophy, an avatar is an embodiment of
the Divine who links God to humans. *Avatar* is also a Sanskrit word
meaning "descent." When water descending from a kitchen faucet is
used for cooking, fire is linked to the functions of human life.

THE COOKING TRIANGLE

In addition to fire and water, the kitchen also needs the stability of earth to be useful. The metal of the stove provides a solid base for igniting fire. It offers a reliable container that directs fire's potentially destructive force toward creative uses. The qualities of earth encircle the stove in the forms of kitchen cabinets, countertops, floors, walls, and ceiling.

A cabinet with a fine mesh screen reveals crockery within.

A freestanding cabinet can be used to store dishes.

Glass doors display the shapes, colors, and textures of dinnerware.

Every manual on kitchen design uses the ubiquitous planning triangle that relates the stove to the sink and the refrigerator. This diagram of efficient function also reveals the archetypal triad that creates a kitchen for the soul—fire, water, and earth. The invisible processes of the soul become tangible forms through the warming passion of fire, the fluid imagination of water, and the firm stability of earth. This triangle cups the psyche, providing a crucible within which the alchemical work of cooking makes a home for the soul.

Kitchen work approached from this perspective allows us to participate in the three elemental forces of nature: creation, preservation, and dissolution. The refrigerator is the center of preservation. The cool interior, sealed in hermetic fashion, fends off decay and promotes freshness. Foods that are not as susceptible to decomposition, such as grains, dried herbs, oils, potatoes, onions, and winter squashes, are maintained in cabinets, drawers, shelves, jars, bags, and

baskets, or are hung from hooks. Displays of fruits and vegetables in baskets and other containers offer functional shrines to the powers that sustain life. Each item of food is a messenger of the cosmos. Sunlight, water, and soil speak to us through carrots, rice, and apples. Bees and flowers send their telegrams through honey, fruits, and berries. The wisdom of ancient gatherers and cultivators of the earth can be read in the colors and textures of rice and legumes.

An Indian spice tin reflects wholeness by organizing spices in a mandala of circles.

Making a meal is a primal act of soulmaking. Few activities delight the soul with such directness and immediacy. Each task of cooking—selecting the ingredients, washing them, chopping or slicing, mixing, and cooking—nourishes a different facet of the soul. Selecting allows us to become aware of the flavors that will delight the soul. Each food contains more than vitamins and minerals; each offers particular qualities of consciousness to savor, such as the sweetness in a string bean, tartness in a raspberry,

Colored and patterned ceramic tiles on a countertop link this kitchen to the sun and earth.

53

Utensils connect mind and body to the preparation of food. The varied shapes and textures of these handles reflect the assortment of thoughts and actions that go into the work.

Above The keen blade of a knife begins transformation, slicing through the rough outer skin to reveal the nourishment within.

Below A grater turns a block of cheese into fine ribbons that are easily blended with other foods.

sourness in a lemon, earthiness in a potato. Washing the food begins the transformation and recalls the ritual purification that begins many sacred observances. The cool water pouring from the kitchen faucet can be soothing and refreshing. While scrubbing the vegetables we can feel the beautiful forms of nature. Cutting, chopping, grating, and grinding are precise movements that allow the skillful interaction of mind and body. These actions break down the separateness and isolation of each ingredient, enabling it to blend with other foods and spices. Each slice reveals amazing colors and shapes. Combining the chopped foodstuffs into new forms by mixing the ingredients in bowls, kneading bread dough, or stirring herbs into soups, we can experience the harmonious blending that begins an act of re-creation. Lighting the burners or heating the oven, we are warmed by the creative fires that transform the prepared recipes into satisfying meals.

UTENSILS

Kitchen utensils and appliances are designed to serve the transformational work of the kitchen triangle. They are tools of the soul, instruments that give body and mind access to the flavors and nourishment hidden within food. With a knife, for example, we can discover the taste of an orange or the sustenance within a butternut squash. Utensils allow fire and water to join in kitchen work. A teakettle facilitates the transmission of heat to water. Sliced carrots stirred in a frying pan with a spoon can receive the transforming powers of the burner's flames. Knives, mortars and pestles, sieves, scales, pots, bowls, bottles, jars, spoons, brushes, brooms, and other kitchen gear are practical symbols for the ways that soul shapes the world into a home.

Knives, Peelers, and Graters

Knives, peelers, and graters allow us to sever and divide. They extend the ability of our hands to draw the essence of food from its enclosing shell. The handle of a well-designed knife is sculpted to fit the shape of the palm and fingers. Its curving form provides an elegant counterpoint to the angular blade. A well-sharpened blade allows the motions of slicing to become fluid and pleasurable. A flash of light on the gleaming steel is a visual sign of the blade's precise edge. Such a knife recalls the keen intellect that can cut to the core of life experience. In Buddhist philosophy, cutting with a knife signifies the liberation attained by slicing through the bonds of ignorance and pride. Peelers strip away the outer skin of fruits and vegetables in curling ribbons, revealing their nourishing inner substance. Graters tear foods into fine particles that are more easily blended and digested. Electric food processors are high-powered versions of these fundamental tools.

Mortar and Pestle

The mortar and pestle crushes herbs and spices into fine powders that permeate food with flavor. The firm hollow of the mortar cradles the brittle, airy leaves of the herbs, framing the deposit of earthy colors and textures. The mortar's rounded porcelain bowl invites the hand to steady it against the grinding action of the pestle. Moving easily along the arched interior of the mortar, the curved end of the pestle grinds the spices, releasing their pungent aromas. The mortar embodies the feminine, receptive principle, and the pestle manifests the masculine force. Together they create a symbol of the stirring of the soul that produces the elixir of life. Mortars and pestles were often depicted in alchemical laboratories to represent the combining of small factors to transform consciousness.

The sieve separates the essential from the superfluous.

Sieve

The sieve is used to purify foods by sifting out the dross and revealing their essence. It recalls the gaining of self-knowledge through discriminating the true self from the false, a freeing of consciousness through selection and choice. In Vedic mythology, the sky is seen as a sieve through which the soma juice flows in drops of fertilizing rain.

Measuring cups facilitate the balanced blending of ingredients in a recipe.

Scales

Scales and measuring cups are tools of balance and proportion. They offer a means of blending ingredients according to the laws of a recipe, the wisdom of combining foods that will please the soul. "A false balance is an abomination to the Lord," states the Old Testament, "but a just weight is his delight." Scales are associated with the astrological sign of Libra, representing the soul qualities of economy, deliberation, and harmony.

Bowls

Diverse shapes and materials create personal expressions of soul.

Bowls embody the feminine, receptive fertility of the Mother Goddess. The weight and texture of a clay mixing bowl allow us to experience this earthy connection. The colors and grain of wooden bowls deepen with age, recording the memories of use in countless meals. In spiritual life, the alms bowl signifies the surrendered and open individual whose bowl is filled with the abundant offerings of nature. At Buddhist shrines, an arrangement of seven bowls represents the seven offerings presented to an honored guest: water for drinking, water for washing, flowers, incense, lighted lamps, clothing, and food. Bowls receive and blend diverse ingredients in preparation for cooking.

Pots and Pans

Pots and pans embody nourishment, sustenance, and abundance. They are emblems of fertility and the magic power of transformation, the death of what goes in and the rebirth of what comes out, as well as the reproductive forces of the earth. In Celtic legend, the magic cauldron of Keridwen has three powers: inexhaustibility, regeneration, inspiration. In alchemy, the pot, or crucible, is seen as the matrix— the receptive feminine used in conjunction with the active, male fire. It is the womb to which all must return before regeneration and rebirth, the place of severe testing and initiatory trials before rebirth into a more expanded state. A dark, weighty cast-iron skillet will stand up to almost any test. Its thick bottom receives intense flames and spreads the heat evenly throughout the pan. The skillet will shed the most caked-on residues of cooked food after a soaking and scouring. The soulful patina of a well-used copper or stainless steel pot deepens and enriches the act of cooking.

Spoons

Spoons and ladles are used in conjunction with bowls, pots, and pans for mixing and serving. Wooden spoons are satisfying to hold. Over time, the friction of stirring countless soups and other dishes sculpts them into unique and personal shapes. In Vedic ceremonies, the spoon is associated with Brahma, the Creator, and Agni, the god of fire and creative intelligence. Blenders and food processors are essentially electrified mixing spoons.

The softened edges and patina of wooden spoons hold the memory of the soulful actions of stirring and serving.

Aprons

The apron in the tradition of Freemasonry is an emblem of craftsmanship. A kitchen apron is used in the craft of cooking. Since aprons are worn during the creation of nourishment, they are symbols of fertility. They also honor the chastity associated with the hearth goddess Hestia and the vestal virgins by covering the genitals and breasts.

Brooms

Brooms embody the magical power of sweeping out unwanted influences.

Brooms, used to sweep every room of a home, are usually stored in or near the kitchen. Since ancient times brooms have been seen as containing magical powers. The theme of the sorcerer's apprentice who transforms a broom into a water carrier dates back to ancient Egypt. During the festival of Anthesteria in ancient Greece, the citizens of Athens invited the souls of the dead into their homes, but then used brooms to drive them out. In Europe, it was thought that life force flowed from the twigs of brooms, which were tied to rooftops to ward off bad weather. The Aztecs celebrated the broom with a festival to Teteo-innan, the earth goddess who swept away disease and harm.

FOOD

Utensils connect our desire for nourishment with the substances of nourishment. In food, we touch, smell, and taste the nuances of soul. Food does more than satisfy our physical hunger. Its flavors and textures also feed our spiritual bodies. Just the thought of a rich, flavorful soup can make a winter day more habitable. A broth with potatoes, carrots, lentils, and herbs not only fills the stomach, it warms the heart and mind.

Milk

Milk is the first food. Immediately after birth our mouths seek nourishment. Milk streams to meet this desire. The fluid flows easily through the sucking mouth and into the stomach; its creaminess satisfies the belly of the soul. Because of this primal connection, milk is used in the initiation ceremonies of many cultures. It is a symbol of the Mother Goddess, food from the gods, and a link to the ancestors. Milk and honey are the foods of paradise. They connect the fertility, harmony, and nourishment-giving of the cow and the industriousness and order of the bee to the tree of the Mother Goddess at the center of paradise. In Christian thought, milk recalls the heavenly milk from the spiritual bride, the Church. Milk and honey were ritually given to the newly baptized. The milk pail is an icon of the spiritual nourishment of Christ. In Buddhism, milk is a symbol of the dharma, conveying a similar notion. The Vedas describe a tree in paradise that yields milk. Milk is so sacred to the bedouins of northern Africa that they consider selling it to be unholy.

Apples

Apples in their roundness embody the totality of the soul. They signify fertility, love, and knowledge. Yet, apples also connote deceitfulness and death. Eating an apple brought Adam and Eve knowledge, but the Bible tells us that this knowledge was gained through the deceit of the serpent. Greek mythology reflects this ambiguity by describing the apple as sacred to Aphrodite; on the other hand, Aphrodite was also given an "apple of discord" by Paris. Perhaps it is because love unites opposites that the apple is a symbol of romance. Part of European courtship involved sending or tossing apples to one's intended lover. When the newlyweds of ancient Athens entered their bridal chambers, they divided and ate an apple before consummating their

The round shape of an apple reflects the completeness of the soul. The pattern of a cut apple recalls the shape of a vulva.

union. In another Greek myth, the fruit becomes an emblem of fertility when Gaia, the earth goddess, gives Hera an apple to enhance fecundity upon her engagement to Zeus. In this regard, apples have been related to women's breasts. The design revealed by an apple cut in two is associated with the vulva. Apples are also linked to bodily health: "An apple a day keeps the doctor away." The Celts saw apples as embodiments of the wisdom handed down from ancestors. Their mythic paradise was called Avalon, meaning Appleland. Europeans placed apples on Christmas trees to indicate that through celebrating the birth of Christ, one can return to a condition of primordial wholeness.

Eggs

An egg is a microcosm of the universe. Its form is seamless, unending. Unlike the static balance of a sphere, the bulging shape of an egg is dynamic. It rises toward transformation. Hidden within the egg is the

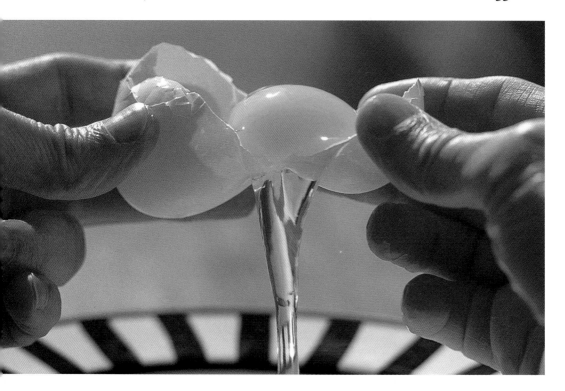

"In the beginning, this world was merely nonbeing. It was existent. It developed. It turned into an egg. . . . It was split asunder. One of the two eggshell parts became silver, one gold. That which was silver is the earth. That which was gold is the sky. What was the outer membrane is the mountains. What was the inner membrane is cloud and mist. What were the veins are the rivers. What was the fluid is the ocean. Now, what was born there from [this egg] is yonder sun."

The Upanishads

germ of creation, the cosmic soup that holds the potential and mystery of new life. Alchemists viewed the egg as a symbol of the sealed hermetic vessel in which the great work of the soul was consummated. Buddhists see the act of breaking through the shell as symbolic of breaking through ignorance to a spiritual rebirth. An old custom in some parts of Europe was to throw an egg over the roof of a house and bury it where it landed to protect the house against lightning.

Bread

Bread is an expression of the development of human culture, a humble food with great symbolic power. It marks the transition from the movable home of the early nomads to the fixed home made possible by farming. Preparing the soil, planting grain, cultivating, reaping, threshing, and baking recall the work of soul transformation. "Breaking bread together" became a sacred rite, and the twelve loaves of shewbread in the Christian tabernacle signify spiritual nourishment. Bread recalls the ritual "bread of life" of the Holy Eucharist. In medieval times, it was popular to bless loaves of bread coming out of the oven with the sign of the cross. In Asia, rice is the symbolic equivalent of bread. The spiritual and material importance of this staple is demonstrated in Japan where the god Inari, the rice bearer, is honored with more than forty thousand shrines.

Corn

Corn symbolizes the abundance produced from the marriage of the sun's rays to the fertile earth, causing the germination of the seed that sustains life. An ear of corn was the key symbol in the Greek mystery schools. As part of their initiation rites, an ear of corn that had been reaped in silence was exhibited as the perfect object of mystic contemplation. The Romans planted corn on the graves of their ancestors to bring the energy and wisdom of their forebears to their daily life.

North American culture relates a similar theme. An Algonquin tale describes a boy who is concerned about his aging father who can no longer hunt. To ease his father's plight, the boy longs for another way of obtaining food. During the night the boy has a vision of a young man with green plumes sprouting out of his head. The young man challenges the boy to a wrestling match. The young man wins, returns for several nights, and wins each time. Finally, the young man tells the boy that the next time they wrestle, the boy must kill him, bury his body, and take care of the burial place. The boy does this, and after some time, returns to find corn growing on the burial plot. Bringing his father to see the miracle, he says, "We no longer need to go out hunting now."

Salt

Salt is a direct representation of the soul. It signifies the indestructibility of the life force, faithfulness, and wisdom. Salt brings out the flavor of food as soulful experience allows us to savor life. As the soul preserves life, salt is used to preserve food. Salt was rubbed on the lips of infants in ancient Rome to ward off danger. Leviticus in the Old Testament declares that salt is to be used as a sacred offering, connecting humans to divine life: "With all thine offerings thou shalt offer salt." Jesus called his followers "the salt of the earth." Alchemists thought that salt linked spirit to matter, that "salt serves to 'fix' the volatile spirit." Salt is also seen as a destructive force. It was scattered across Carthage by the conquering Romans to make the soil barren forever. Lot's wife, upon seeing the destruction of Sodom and Gomorrah, became a pillar of salt.

Fish

Fish represent the unconscious desires that rise from the depths of the soul to the surface of conscious awareness. They are also fertility symbols and are associated with many goddesses of love. Since they are "cold-blooded," however, they are "not governed by the heat of passion," making them prime candidates for sacred purposes. The Vedic god Vishnu, preserver and savior of the world, first incarnated as a fish, marking the beginning of the present age. This image directly corresponds to the Christian use of the fish as a symbol of Christ.

Honey

Honey epitomizes the sweetness of the soul. The wisdom consumed by prophets is described in Ezekiel as being as "sweet as honey." The promised land of Exodus is said to be "flowing with milk and honey." When the Old Testament Samson tore apart a lion with his bare hands, honey and a swarm of bees poured out of the carcass, symbolizing the new life that emerges from death. In ancient China, honey was spread on the lips of the god of the kitchen to encourage the deity to speak sweetly when he made his annual report to heaven about the inhabitants of the house.

COOKING A MEAL

Enhance the soulfulness of cooking a meal by preparing it in the following way. Before going to the market, imagine a recipe with aromas and flavors that will delight the spirit as well as feed your family. After bringing home the ingredients, set the raw foods, herbs, and spices for the meal on a counter. Discard all paper and plastic wrapping. Instead of immediately plunging into action, pause for a moment to savor the colors, textures, and aromas of each ingredient. If a homemade marinara sauce for pasta is your choice, focus your awareness on the tomatoes' smooth, shiny redness next to the bell pepper's brilliant green, the carrot's deep orange, and the papery white of the garlic. Breathe in the fragrances of the basil, thyme, parsley, and bay leaves.

Next, place the utensils for cooking the meal on the counter beside the collection of ingredients. Note how the form and material of each utensil will assist in preparing the meal—how the knife handle is molded to fit the hand, how the serrated blade severs the tomatoes.

In cooking a meal, place, utensils, and raw foodstuffs are combined in a soulmaking process.

Treat each step in preparing the meal as a small ceremony. Wash the tomatoes, bell pepper, carrot, celery, and parsley as an act of purification that not only prepares the food for the meal but also prepares you for the work. As you chop the vegetables, observe the colors and fragrances that are released by the blade of the knife. Heating the oil, scooping the mounds of chopped ingredients into the saucepan, and stirring in the garlic, basil, thyme, and parsley, be mindful of how combining the different foods transforms them into a new form of sustenance. Drawing water for the pasta and placing it on the burner, notice how the energy of fire is transmitted to the water and how the bubbling liquid then changes the dry, brittle pasta into pliant, flavorful food. As the sauce is cooking, clean the counter in preparation for serving.

ARRANGING A SOULFUL KITCHEN

These observations of the kitchen suggest a number of motifs that can enrich the soulfulness of your kitchen. Arrange the area around the stove so that it invites you to engage in the transformations of cooking. Hang pots, pans, and utensils within easy reach of the stove—on the wall next to the stove or from overhead pot racks. Place spices so they are close at hand in clear containers. Make these displays lively and beautiful by using the varied shapes, colors, and materials of the pans and utensils to create a sculptural display. Hang wreaths of dried herbs and flowers in this area.

Honor fire by decorating the cooking area with medallions and plaques of the sun, or pictures of solar gods and primal fire. Use fiery colors on the walls or in ceramic tiles surrounding the stove. Look for tiles that are decorated with solar designs and use them as trivets; the warm, earthy color of a small Mexican paver backed with felt is also good for this use. If there is a window near the stove, place pieces of stained glass or prisms on the sill to catch the sunlight and transform it into colorful designs.

Remember the transforming power of time with pictures or tiles that depict the four seasons or times of the day. Salt and pepper shakers can have unusual designs that can be changed with the seasons. A friend gave us a set of shakers in the shape of turkeys for use at Thanksgiving and rabbits for the spring. As a reminder of the interplay of fire and water in cooking, leave a kettle filled with water on the stove.

If the stove embodies mythic images of solar fire, the sink embodies images of the moon and water. Near the sink, use design motifs of

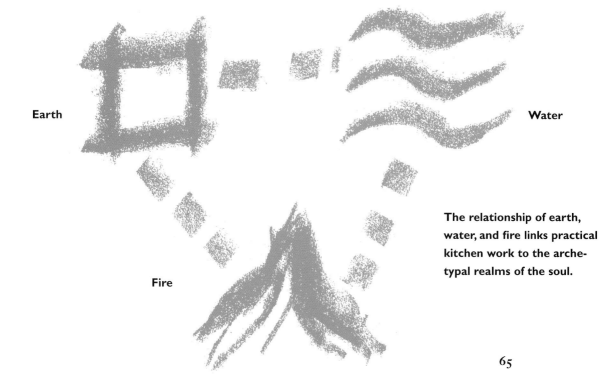

Earth

Water

Fire

The relationship of earth, water, and fire links practical kitchen work to the archetypal realms of the soul.

lunar deities, clouds, rain, and the ocean. Mirrors, glazed tiles with reflective finishes, objects of blue or green glass, and other gleaming materials can be used to enhance the sparkling qualities of water. Hang dish towels nearby that have watery colors and/or designs. Use natural sponges, and brushes with wooden instead of plastic handles. Place seashells, river rocks, or stones worn by the sea near the sink. Hang a pot scrubber on a hook by the sink so it's ready for use.

Arrange the storage area to honor the preservation of food. Use glass cabinet doors or open shelving to display the color, shape, and texture of foodstuffs. Organize these foodstuffs according to color, creating a spectrum of hues. Place lighting within cabinets and shelving to illuminate the stored food as you would objects of art. Store grains, pasta, and dried beans in glass containers or jars. Hang herbs, peppers, and other dried ingredients from hooks. Place fruit and squashes in bowls and baskets. If you collect unusual dishes, coffee mugs, or other items, create special shelving to display them.

Add beauty to the refrigerator by using unexpected storage containers such as a nestlike basket for eggs or an earthy bowl for vegetables. Use glass containers instead of plastic. Reduce the sterile feeling in the refrigerator by placing unusual containers or stones, driftwood, or seed pods inside, taking care that small children do not mistake these for edibles.

REMODELING OR BUILDING A NEW KITCHEN

An existing room can be remodeled into a soulful kitchen in the following ways. Begin by observing the unique qualities of the room you are going to remodel. Notice its shape and proportions. A tall room offers possibilities for a vaulted or peaked ceiling, or tall windows. See how the room relates to adjacent rooms. You may want to open or close off the relationship to other rooms. Look at the windows, their size, shape, and placement. Notice the views and imagine whether you want to highlight them or not. Observe the qualities of light at the times of the day that you usually use the kitchen. Look for any other features that give this room its particular personality, such as a wood-plank floor or unusual moldings.

Imagine cooking a meal in this room. Think of where you might place the stove, sink, refrigerator, and storage units. Walk through the steps of preparing a meal within this cooking triangle. Notice how this arrangement supports a smooth flow of action or impedes it. Imagine other arrangements and see if they are an improvement on your first layout. If you live in a single-family dwelling, think of how you might add windows to add sunlight and views.

Think of the materials and colors that you associate with soulful cooking—earthy tones and textures or refined hues and fibers. Imagine the cabinets, appliances, flooring, and wall covering that reflect soul. Look in magazines, kitchen stores, and remodeling centers for the materials that have these qualities. Look for a stove that has a soulful character—thick prongs on the burners; solid, hefty control knobs; and a color other than white. Install cabinets made of natural wood, or painted cabinets that are colorful or uniquely designed. Cabinets stenciled with motifs that portray the transforming interaction of fire, water, and earth described earlier in this chapter are a possibility. Choose a refrigerator that can be paneled with wood that matches your cabinet doors. Some refrigerators have glass doors that allow food to be displayed. Make your countertops thirty inches deep instead of the standard twenty-four; this will allow you to display food and utensils on the counter and still have uncluttered work space. Use granite or butcher block as countertops. Consider brick, clay tile, or wood flooring to give a feeling of warmth.

If you are building a new home, think of the importance you want to give the kitchen. If the kitchen plays a central role, place it near the center of your plan. If it is peripheral, place it near the edges. Imagine how you would like the kitchen to relate to the surrounding environment, such as facing the morning sun or a particular view or opening onto a terrace.

Architects seem to design for themselves last. When I do design my own kitchen, it will look like this: My ideal kitchen for the soul is a rectangular room measuring approximately twelve feet by sixteen feet. A vaulted ceiling overhead rests on off-white plaster walls. One end of the room frames the sink. The deep bowl of stone or porcelain is topped with a gooseneck faucet of aged brass. The sink faces an expanse of windows that follow the arched line of the vaulted ceiling. The deep sills of these windows hold potted plants and herbs. At the other end of the room, French doors open to the dining room. The stove, with heavy steel burners and oven doors, is set into an arched alcove on one side of the room. Heavy stainless steel pots hang above the stove. The cabinets are custom designed to accommodate the cooking habits of our household. They are made of bird's-eye maple and have a combination of glass doors and doors that are stenciled with geometric patterns that portray the sun, moon, and plant motifs. Wooden panels of this design cover the refrigerator door so that it blends in. The countertops and backsplash are made of Dakota Crazy Horse granite, containing earthy hues of red and gray. The edge of the countertop is one and a half inches thick with an ogee shape. The floor is made of eight-inch squares of French limestone set in a diagonal pattern. Lighting on top of the cabinets illuminates the vaulted ceiling, casting an indirect glow over the room. Task lighting is concealed underneath the cabinets. An arched niche near the entry to the kitchen frames a ceramic bowl filled with apples, winter squash, or other foods.

5

Dining Rooms

THE HUNGER OF THE SOUL MEETS THE FULLNESS OF CRE-
ATION IN THE DINING ROOM; THE TRANSFORMATIVE FIRE
OF THE KITCHEN BECOMES THE FIRE OF DIGESTION.
HUNGER MOTIVATES OUR THOUGHTS, WORDS, AND
ACTIONS. WE HUNGER FOR LOVE, HAPPINESS, FOOD, AND
NUMEROUS OTHER THINGS. THE DINING ROOM OFFERS
THE SOUL A SEAT WHERE THESE INNER CRAVINGS CAN
RECEIVE NOURISHMENT. "THE SEAT OF THE SOUL IS THERE
WHERE THE INNER AND OUTER WORLDS MEET," WROTE
THE EIGHTEENTH-CENTURY GERMAN POET NOVALIS.

Eating is one of the central images of spiritual understanding. In the Garden of Eden, Adam and Eve are urged by a serpent to eat fruit from the tree of the knowledge of good and evil. In doing so, Adam and Eve engage in the processes of life. As Joseph Campbell points out in *The Power of Myth:* "Life consists in eating other creatures. You don't think about that very much when you're eating a nice meal. But what you're doing is eating something that was recently alive [animal or vegetable]. When you look at the beauty of nature . . . you see the [animals] eating things. . . . The serpent is a traveling alimentary canal, that's about all it is. And it gives you that primary sense of shock, of life in its most primal quality. Life lives by killing and eating itself, casting off death and being reborn."

Eating is a primal pursuit of the soul. Hunger is as much spiritual as it is physical. The mysterious paradox that life continues by consuming life is an essential part of sacred practices. The act of Jesus breaking bread, sharing it with his disciples, and saying, "Eat this. This is my flesh," is the theme of the Eucharist. During Holy Communion, Catholics regard the wine and wafer as symbols of the blood and body of Christ. In the Thomas Gospel, Jesus says, "He who drinks from my mouth will become as I am, and I shall be he." By our becoming aware of the connection between food and spirit, our daily meals can become a means of communing with the soul.

Bodily hunger compels us to eat, but psychological and spiritual hunger are larger than our physical appetites. Food feeds the stomach, but it primarily nourishes the soul. On a cold, winter day, the warm coziness of a richly flavored stew dominates the soul's cravings more than the carbohydrates and proteins needed by the body. In summer, the soul may long for a dish of ice cream even though it has little nutritional value. Anxiety, loneliness, and other emotions urge us to reach for "hug" foods such as pizza or cookies, hoping to fill an inner void.

Flatware of stainless steel, brass, and wood, and floral-patterned table linens, add richness to this meal.

DINNERWARE

Each furnishing and houseware in the dining room embodies the hollowness that thirsts for nourishment, both material and spiritual. The circular, concave shapes of bowls and plates are designed to receive the fruits of kitchen work. Their gracefully rounded rims invite food to fill the inner recesses. The alms bowl of a monk represents his surrender to the void within the material world and his readiness to

A dining area in the kitchen recalls the age-old custom of enjoying a meal near the glow of the hearth.

receive spiritual fullness from the soul. Spoons and forks extend our cravings into material form, reaching into the basins of plates and bowls and drawing nourishment to the mouth.

Cups and glasses receive fluid forms of nourishment. They are like the open heart, receiving, containing, and pouring life blood into the whole body. In this regard, the chalice and the Holy Grail are symbols of the cosmic heart of creation. They contain the waters of life, the inexhaustible source of sustenance and abundance. Drinking from a cup is an act of absorbing life and power. In many cultures, drinking from the same cup is a ritual of marriage and unity among friends.

A thick plank of oak with a rough-hewn edge by Duncan MacMaster connects the meals eaten at this table with nature.

TABLES, CHAIRS, AND SIDEBOARDS

The table is an open, spreading surface that honors and upholds plates, bowls, and dinnerware. It displays the fruits of nature and the inner workings of the spirit that transform raw materials into nourishing sustenance. Square and rectangular tables honor the four directions of sacred space—north, south, east, and west. Round tables reflect the circular movements of the heavens, wholeness, and totality. The twelve knights of King Arthur's Round Table represent the twelve signs of the zodiac. Round tables also depict equality, since there is no head or foot.

Setting candles on a table brings the vitalizing power of fire, light, and the radiance of consciousness to a meal. In the Cabala, three candles placed together signify wisdom, strength, and beauty. A chandelier hung over the table or a candelabra placed on the table embodies the tree of life in full bloom.

The height of a table has a profound impact on our experience of dining. In the West, sitting on chairs at a table is taken for granted. In the East, most people sit on cushions at low tables. Gathering for a meal at a low table can bring a more grounded and intimate feeling to the enjoyment of a meal.

Chairs provide raised, receptive hollows for sitting and receiving food. The word *chair* comes from the Greek *kathedra*, or seat, and is the root of the word *cathedral*. A cathedral is a sanctuary for opening our awareness to the mysteries of creation. A chair at the dining table becomes a little cathedral where we can awaken to the miraculous web of life that allows food to be brought to the table and we can experience direct communion with the vital powers of nature. In Vedic architecture, the square seat of a chair is related to the sacred square that forms the ground plan of the temple. As the material form of wholeness, the square embodies the pairs of opposites that balance and turn the wheel of life—order and chaos, knowledge and ignorance. Positive forces are depicted by the vertical legs of the chair, and the horizontal shafts that tie the legs together depict negative forces.

Sideboards hold and display prepared meals. They provide altars for savoring the gifts of the fields and the work of the kitchen. Sideboards display and honor the utensils of dining: platters, serving spoons, candles, and other objects.

A rectangular table gathers sustenance from the four sacred directions.

Rich woods and earthy textures invite the soul to dwell in this dining room.

MEALS

Food fills hunger and thirst with the fullness of creation. Each morsel is a representative of the universe. A carrot, for example, is the culmination of innumerable processes and circumstances. The season of the year, sun, rain, soil, human labor, knowledge of plant cultivation, wisdom of food preparation, the economic system that brings sustenance to the table, and countless other factors combine to create a meal. The cornucopia or horn of plenty is an ancient symbol signifying endless bounty and fertility. The cornucopia's shape displays the paradox of creativity and receptivity that produce the fruitfulness of nature. It is at once a horn and a hollow basket, a phallus and a womb.

Eating allows us to imbibe the myriad qualities of food. More than mere nutriments, we consume the textures, flavors, aromas, colors, sounds, and spirit of the foods we eat. A crisp green salad contains different vitamins and minerals than an enchilada; it also provides a different sensory and emotional experience. The salad is an airy realm of crunchy freshness; the enchilada, an earthy world of soft spiciness.

The characteristics of the meals we consume enliven dormant qualities of the soul. Cooling foods, such as cucumbers or oranges,

tend to cool the psyche and the body; hot foods, such as jalapeño peppers or ginger, can make us "hotheaded" and energetic. Food can urge us to feel heavy or light, dry or moist, sour or sweet, salty or bland.

Look for a moment at the food you are eating and you can perceive the miracle of creation, the impulses of the soul taking physical form. Within a plate of steaming pasta are the deities of fire, water, and earth—the hearth flame of Hestia, the thunderbolts and rain clouds of Zeus, and the fertile grains of Demeter. The guiding wisdom of the earth mother Gaia is there along with the primal desire for more in life and the opportunity to find fullness. The ancient mystery religions understood this when they made fish, bread, and wine their sacramental meal. Fish signify physical matter enlivened by the spirit rising from the depths of the soul. The intoxicating power of wine makes it a messenger of divine ecstasy. Bread symbolizes the immortality of the spirit; the wheat dies as it is harvested and rises again in life-giving loaves.

Eating is also akin to spiritual transformation. Biting breaks through the boundaries of matter. Tasting, we become conscious of our specific relationship with the physical world; we learn to discriminate between what is nourishing and what is not, and become aware of the subtle flavors and textures of creation. Chewing integrates mind and body; our digestive juices dissolve the hard boundaries of matter. Swallowing unifies inner and outer, soul and matter.

ENJOYING A MEAL

Mealtime is an opportunity to gather with family and friends. Besides the soulfulness in the food, there is soulfulness within the people who gather. Even if we eat alone, we can pause and see a universe of wonder within the food. Saying grace is a way of appreciating the food and those we are gathered with. Having a moment of silence or saying a

Saying grace provides an opportunity to reconnect with the silence of the soul.

few words of appreciation for the meal allows mind and body to savor the gift of life in the present moment. The heart can open in gratitude and we can prepare ourselves to be fully enriched by the food and conversation. We can remember that we are not alone but are interconnected with the rest of creation. Almost every spiritual tradition offers words of thanks that reflect this theme. Here are a few examples:

Bless our hearts
to hear in the
breaking of the bread the
song of the universe.

Father John Giulliani

Blessed art Thou, O Lord our God, King of the universe,
who creates many living beings and the things they need.
For all that thou hast created to sustain the life of every living being,
blessed be Thou, Life of the universe.

Rabbi Hayim Halevy Donin

In Thy fullness, my Lord,
Filled with Thy grace,
For the purpose of union with Thee
And to satisfy and glorify Thy creation,
With thanks to Thee with all our hearts
And with all our love for Thee,
With all adoration for Thy blessings
We accept this food as it has come to us.
The food is Thy blessing and in Thy service
We accept in all gratitude, my Lord.

Maharishi Mahesh Yogi

Everyone at the table join hands for a silent moment.

Quaker Grace

Thich Nhat Hanh in *Peace Is Every Step* offers the following suggestions for eating a meal together:

- Turn off the TV, put down the newspaper, and work together for five or ten minutes, setting the table and finishing whatever needs to be done.

- When the food is on the table and everyone is seated, breathe in and out three times.

- Then, look at each person as you breathe in and out to be in touch with yourself and everyone at the table. "We don't need two hours to see another person. If we are really settled within ourselves, we only need to look for one or two seconds, and that is enough to see. . . . Sitting at the table with other people, we have a chance to offer an authentic smile of friendship and understanding. It is very easy, but not many people do it. If the people in a household cannot smile at each other, the situation is very dangerous."

- After breathing and smiling, look down at the food in a way that allows it to become real. The extent to which the food nourishes us depends on us. We can see and taste the whole universe in a piece of bread.

Hanh continues with the following observation: "Having the opportunity to sit with our family and friends and enjoy wonderful food is something precious, something not everyone has. Many people in the world are hungry. When I hold a bowl of rice or piece of bread, I know that I am fortunate, and I feel compassion for all those who have no food to eat and are without friends or family."

When you have finished the meal, gather the dishes together with mindfulness. Enjoy creating order by placing the flatware in a common bowl, stacking the dishes neatly, and arranging the glasses on a tray before carrying them into the kitchen. Notice the colors and shapes of the objects that were used to create the centerpiece. Enjoy the textures of the tablecloth or place mats and napkins. When the

table has been completely cleared, pause for a moment to appreciate how you were nourished by the food and friendship gathered around the dining room table.

ARRANGING A SOULFUL DINING ROOM

My wife, Suzanne, makes the dining table a sacred setting in a number of ways. She uses tablecloths that reflect the time of year—bright patterns and colors in spring, pastels in summer, and warm, earthy tones in autumn and winter. She spreads a runner down the center of the table bordered by place mats that mark each setting. She may use a different place mat at each setting to honor the individuality of the person who will use it. Sometimes she creates natural place mats with a scattering of autumn leaves, or wild grasses.

Suzanne designs centerpieces that honor the time of day and year. Flowers floating in a bowl of water create a cooling influence for a summer noontime meal. A cluster of candles ringed by a wreath of dried flowers, pinecones, nuts, or winter squashes warms a winter evening table. Flat stones and seashells make interesting, organic candle holders. She puts tiny bottles as vases at each place setting, filling them with a single flower or sprig of herb.

She uses plates and bowls that integrate with the flavors, colors, and textures of the meal being served—earthenware for ethnic dishes, delicate china for haute cuisine, a geometric design for nouvelle repasts. She might place a different style or color plate at each setting to reflect the personality of the individual using it.

Suzanne uses napkin rings of jute or raffia. She sometimes encourages the use of chopsticks, which help to slow the pace of a meal and provide more texture than metal forks and spoons. For chopstick holders, pieces of driftwood, stones, seashells, and other natural objects are used; these items are also offered as pedestals for flatware.

A centerpiece creates an altarlike setting, adding sacredness to a meal.

Instead of using goblets or drinking glasses, beverages are served in ceramic bowls, making the drinking of water, tea, juice, or wine more conscious and reverent.

Sideboards are arranged according to the theme of the meal. Extra raw ingredients that were not used in preparation—vegetables, spices, grains, etc.—are arranged as decorations by placing them in a beautiful basket or bowl. Other decorations are related to the theme of the centerpiece. As with the plates and bowls, serving platters reflect the flavors, colors, and textures of the meal. Beverages are provided in earthen pitchers or bowls with ladles. A copy of a mealtime prayer or grace might be framed and displayed on the sideboard. These graces are changed to reflect the season or your mood of the day. When it is not being used for a meal, Suzanne will put on the sideboard a book opened to sumptuous photographs of food.

REMODELING OR BUILDING A NEW DINING ROOM

When remodeling or building, consider the following ways of creating a soulful dining room. If you are remodeling, observe the qualities of the present dining room—shape and proportion; connection to adjacent rooms; size and placement of windows; qualities of light; and other features.

Begin the design of a remodeled dining room or a new one by imagining eating a meal in this room. Envision the placement of the table and chairs, sideboard, lighting, and other features. Think of the meals that will be eaten here on different occasions—Thanksgiving and other holidays; family get-togethers; quiet meals for two, etc. Walk through the steps of enjoying a meal in this room—presenting the food, serving it, eating, and cleaning up.

Think of ways you might alter the existing room or shape the new one to support soulful dining. An octagonal or oval dining room would enhance the focus on a central placement of table and chairs. Large windows or French doors would open the dining room to the cycles of nature.

Think of the materials and colors that you associate with soulful dining. An oak or pine floor with wide planks and rough plaster walls adds an earthy flavor; a maple floor of two-and-one-quarter-inch strips and wallpaper conveys refinement. Imagine the table that would best support these activities—its size, material, and design. Do the same with the chairs and sideboard. Look in magazines and furniture stores for the table, chairs, and sideboard that reflect these qualities.

Look for a table with rich wood grain, a weighty top, and substantial legs. Find one that has interesting details at the edge of the tabletop, where the legs meet the top, and where the legs meet the floor. Follow similar guidelines for buying dining chairs. To support the unique characters of family members, select chairs of varied design that reflect the individuality of each person—a geometric chair for one who prefers order and clarity; a chair with flowing curves for one who enjoys organic forms; a high-tech chair for a computer whiz. Consider a low table with cushions for seating.

To add depth and richness, use a wooden chair rail—a strip of molding or paneling thirty inches tall. Instead of placing a chandelier over the table, install wall sconces or torchères to create soft, indirect lighting. Use "food" colors such as reds and greens as accents on the walls, rugs, and other elements.

My ideal dining area? A circular room fifteen feet in diameter with a shallow, domed ceiling. Twelve oak pillars, for the months of the year, ring the room in the plaster enclosing walls. An oak cornice atop the pillars is fitted with concealed bulbs for indirect lighting. Windows to the south open to sunlight, air, and views. A wide niche between the pillars to the north frames a built-in sideboard of quartersawn oak. Openings between the pillars to the west lead to the gathering room; to the east, similar openings lead to the kitchen. At the apex of the domed ceiling is the stenciled design of the sun. Surrounding the sun are images of eight phases of the moon. The floor is made of two-and-one-quarter-inch-wide strips of hickory placed in a pattern of concentric squares radiating out from the center. A square, wool rug with motifs of plants and animals is on the floor. A circular oak table stands on a circular granite base at the center of the room. Comfortable oak chairs ring the table.

6

Gathering Rooms

"I chiseled the names of my paternal ancestors on three stone tablets and placed them in the courtyard of the Tower. I painted the ceiling with motifs from my own and my wife's [family coat of] arms. When I was working on the tablets, I became aware of the fateful links between me and my ancestors. I feel very strongly that I am under the influence of things or questions which were left incomplete and unanswered by my parents and grandparents and more distant ancestors."

C. G. Jung in *Memories, Dreams and Reflections*

Each of us is the continuation of a river of soul flowing from the ancient past. The DNA that guides the growth of cells in our bodies was handed from generation to generation. Wisdom and practical know-how were passed from parent to child for thousands of years. The language we use, the values that shape our worldview, and the habits that guide our actions are the legacy we inherited from those who came before us.

The gathering area is a setting that honors and celebrates what we have received from the past and what we want to create for the future. It is the place of memory and creation, the place where personal and cultural lore is shared with family members and friends. Storytelling, music, dance, art, and games form the language we use to make these transmissions.

In this sense, the gathering room is the abode of Hermes, the Greek messenger god. Hermes supports the fertility that spawns family life from one generation to the next. He clears the roads of stones so travelers may arrive at our door. Hermes is a consummate storyteller. He created music by fashioning the first lyre from a tortoise shell. His winged staff, the caduceus, is entwined by two snakes, symbols of reconciliation between the opposing or diverse forces that can arise when people gather together.

Storytelling is one of the essential purposes for gathering. Since ancient times people have drawn together to exchange news, gossip, knowledge, and insight. Hunters related their exploits, farmers shared know-how, shamans explained the creation of the world and the activities of the gods, families shared the happenings of the day.

FIREPLACES, CONVERSATION, AND TELEVISION

From the earliest human gatherings to the era of radio and television, the setting for transmitting family and cultural lore was the gathering place defined by the fireplace, chimney, and semicircle of seating. In

Symmetrical seating areas create focal points for gathering.

the cold darkness of night, the heat and light of fire established a focal point for gathering. Crackling flames and glowing embers provided a captivating backdrop for transmitting the wisdom of human existence. The chimney carried the fire's smoke skyward, symbolically linking the stories of human life on earth to the mythic tales of the gods in heaven. The image of Santa Claus bringing gifts down the chimney conveys the possibility of spontaneously receiving boons from heaven rather than through the earthly doorway of the workaday world.

The fire and a semicircle of seating is an archetypal setting for passing knowledge and wisdom from generation to generation.

Sitting in a semicircular arrangement allowed those gathered by the fireplace to share the warmth of the flames and simultaneously face one another to discuss family and cultural experiences. This arc of gathering fostered dialogue that could open human consciousness to greater knowledge and wisdom.

Present-day gathering rooms, however, have lost the primal connection between the fireplace, chimney, and semicircle of seating. The soulful habit of hunkering down together, tending the sacred fire, and discussing the mundane and mythic events of life has too often been traded for the dull repose of reclining on the sofa and flicking the television's remote control. We face the blue glow of the television, which illuminates the current affairs of celebrities, politicians, and sitcom characters, instead of facing one another to shed the light of consciousness on the stories of our own lives.

Television plays an important role in contemporary life, but the first step in creating a gathering place for the soul is to remove it from center stage. Putting the television behind the doors of a cabinet or under the veil of a cloth and watching it only on special occasions can bring more consciousness to its use and remind us to engage in activities that nourish the soul.

A new form of gathering has been created by on-line computer communications. Instead of assembling around the glowing flames of a wood fire, we can link up with others through the luminous electronic sparks of information traveling from one computer terminal to another. Communicating in this way, however, does little to nourish the soul. Access to more information gives the illusion that we are endowed with increased wisdom. In reality, the Internet is simply a high-powered tool for communicating bits of information. The totality of experience created by two or more people in the same room cannot be duplicated by a computer. The subtle messages expressed by body language and tone of voice are lost in electronic hookups.

This upright piano provides an altarlike setting for family pictures and mementos.

MUSIC

After storytelling and conversation, the rhythms and melodies of music have been a powerful force for bringing people together. Drums and other percussion instruments pulsate with the cadences of the heartbeat, walking, and the cycles of nature. The human voice, wind instruments, and stringed instruments sing the moods of the soul. Woodwinds such as flutes have long been associated with extremes of emotion. The flute

89

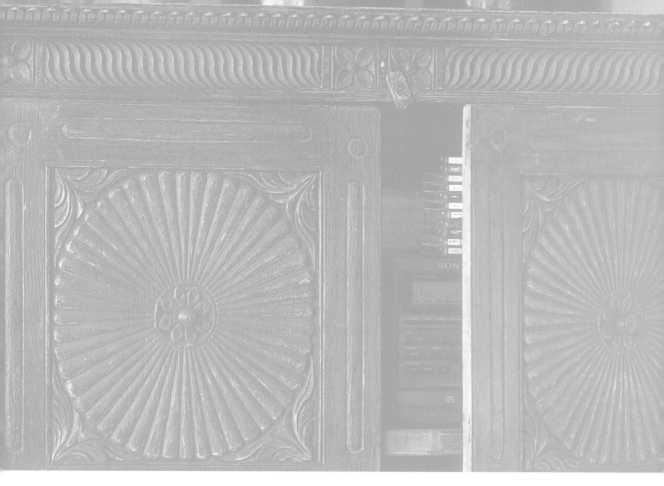

An antique chest provides a beautiful container for stereo equipment and recordings.

of the Indian god Krishna is likened to the voice of eternity crying to the dwellers in time. Stringed instruments such as the lute, lyre, and guitar are emblems of harmony. The Greeks portrayed Orpheus as the good shepherd whose lute charmed wild beasts and resolved conflict. Gandharvaved, the Indian art of classical music, uses music to attune human life with the cycles of nature. Different rhythms and melodies,

**Music allows a gathering to be filled with
the rhythms and melodies of the soul.**

ragas, are played at different times of the day and year to harmonize our moods with the environmental changes that are occurring.

The variety of music now available allows the full spectrum of soul expression to be stirred into the atmosphere of our homes. We can be moved by music from all corners of the globe and many periods in history. A room can be shaped by the baroque soul of Bach or the tropical mystery of Bali, the songs of Nashville or Nigeria, the rhythm of Motown or the chants of the Middle Ages.

Creating our own music with instruments and/or our voices is an ancient way of experiencing soulful gathering. Instead of always being passively entertained, we can use music to engage family members and friends. Singing simple songs together can reconnect us to the soul of our traditions or allow us to appreciate the heritage of others. Melody and rhythm are direct methods for experiencing harmonious gathering.

DANCE

Dancing vibrates the power of music deep into our bones. Through rhythmic movements of the body, the pulsations of the soul take physical form. Our actions in space move with the swing of time. Dancing imitates the rhythms of the cosmos and the divine play of creation. Round dances traditionally reflect the path of the sun, moon, and stars and define a sacred circle of gathering. An object placed at the center of a circular dance is guarded and energized. The Apocryphal Acts of Saint John describe the twelve apostles dancing in a circle around Jesus. In India, Krishna and his consort, Radha, stand at the center of a circle of dancing cowherdesses. The dance of Shiva is said to create and dissolve the universe. In Europe, during the Middle Ages, labyrinth dances were enacted to ward off evil and strengthen a central object. Sometimes a maiden stood at the center of the labyrinth; the dance through the twisting path represented her journey toward paradise. The whirling dervishes of the Mideast imitate the spinning of a planet on its axis and the cycles of existence

turning on the axis of the soul. Dances that form chains or lines are said to express the linking of masculine and feminine powers, connecting the pulse of heaven with the meter of earth.

Traditionally, dancing took place in community settings outside the home. Musicians were needed to create the rhythms and melodies that guided a group through socially prescribed dance steps and movements. Modern stereo equipment and recordings provide access to music any time of the day or night. Freedom from traditional forms of dance allows us to dance alone or with a small group. Creating an area in your gathering room where your body can move to the rhythm and harmony of music offers a direct and immediate experience of soul.

Through dance the body can swing to the music of the soul.

The mythic struggle between light and dark is reenacted by the movement of the pieces on a wooden chess table.

GAMES

Games offer another means of deepening the communion of soul experience. They give us the opportunity to play within specified rules and can often embody the patterns and activity of sacred experience.

Chess, for example, depicts the royal game of life. In *The Illustrated Encyclopaedia of Traditional Symbols*, J. C. Cooper writes that chess, which originated in India, describes the battle between the spiritual powers of light and dark struggling for domination of the world. The checkered board symbolizes the alternating pull of the fundamental dualities of creation—positive/negative, day/night, sun/moon, male/female, clarity/obscurity, time/space, and the crisscrossing pattern of life alternating between fortune and misfortune. The sixty-four squares depict the mandala that formed the ground plan of temples and cities. This design was said to symbolize totality by depicting the infinite possibilities of the cosmos and human life. Chess was used as a meditation ritual in the Buddhist festival of the full moon. The movements of the various pieces outline the movements of soul in the physical world. The king represents the sun, the heart, and the forces of law and order. His moves are limited by the boundaries of life. The queen is the spirit, who moves at will like the moon. The bishop represents rulers of the spiritual world, and his diagonal movement is based on the triangle. His moves on the white squares symbolize the intellectual path of wisdom, and moves on the dark squares indicate the devotional path of the heart. The bishop's triangular passages along one color or the other are linked to the receptive, feminine principle. The rook or castle is the ruler of the world. Its movement is based on the square, the symbol of the earth and material form. The straight movement of the rook denotes virile, masculine energies. The knight uses both the intellectual and devotional way but without the power of the spirit. The jump of the knight's move is likened to the jump of intuition. Pawns are peasants attempting to cross the board through seven grades of initiation to reach the eighth square, signifying the goal of totality, paradise regained, enlightenment, and the ability to move at will.

Playing cards also hold symbolic significance. The fifty-two cards in the deck replicate the fifty-two weeks of the year. The thirteen cards in each suit represent the thirteen lunar months in a year. The four suits stand for the four elements, directions, winds, seasons, and corners of the archetypal temple. The two red suits signify the two warm seasons and the powers of light. The two black suits symbolize the two cold seasons and the powers of darkness. The four designs on the cards are emblems of life. Spades denote the leaf and the cosmic tree, hearts the life center and the world navel, diamonds the feminine principle, and clubs the masculine. The ace is indivisible unity. The king is the spirit, essence, and father. The queen is the soul, personality, and mother. The jack is the ego and the messenger. Together the king, queen, and jack represent the spiritual Trinity.

Artwork
and personal
mementos
enhance the
sacredness
of a
gathering.

ARTWORK AND SACRED OBJECTS

Artwork and personal objects also serve to bring people together. Photographs and other mementos of family members, friends, and meaningful places can reflect soulful connections among family and group members. By honoring the people, customs, and cultural traditions that have enriched us, we can experience the continuum of the soul—the power of the spirit to survive the changes life brings.

Paintings and sculpture can distill a vast range of human experience into powerful images of the spirit. Common objects become sacred when they are invested with personal meaning. During the workshops I conduct, I often ask the participants to bring sacred objects to share with the group. I am always inspired to see how simple objects—a stone from a memorable day at the beach, a wedding ring, or a coffee cup—can become the repository of our most intimate thoughts and experiences.

In recent years floral wreaths have become popular home decorations. Traditionally the circular form of wreaths has expressed numerous qualities of the soul. Wreaths connote glory, victory, holiness, and happiness. They can also signify death and mourning. Bridal wreaths signify virginity and the beginnings of a new life. In Arabia, a wreath of orange blossoms was worn by brides as a sign of fertility; in Greece and Rome, brides wore wreaths of hawthorn or verbena. A wreath of oak leaves was presented as a reward for saving a life. Military heroes were given wreaths of grass. A wreath of roses was worn by Roman emperors.

GATHERING

Gathering can become more soulful in a number of ways. Instead of watching television, organize a reading or storytelling group. Choose a story that everyone knows and see how you can embellish and exaggerate it to make it more fantastic, funny, or inspiring than the last time you told it. Read plays, poems, and inspiring writings. Make up a story on the spot by starting with one person inventing an opening line and each person taking a turn expanding the story.

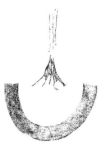

ARRANGING A SOULFUL GATHERING ROOM

Encourage soulfulness in your gathering room by seating people to face one another. U-shaped arrangements of sofas and chairs urge conversation and storytelling. A circle of cushions on the floor can make a gathering feel interconnected and whole. Extradeep sofas and chairs allow sitting cross-legged or in other relaxed postures and make gathering less formal. Plush cushions and textured fabrics such as raw silk and cotton make seating more cozy and intimate.

Include a bookshelf that can be filled with books of stories and plays, making it easy to have readings that delight, inspire, and inform.

Use music to enrich the moods of the day and season. Vary the type of music you listen to in the morning and at night to harmonize with the changing qualities of activity and sunlight. Listen to music that echoes the season of the year. Use musical instruments as decorative objects. Flutes, bells, drums, and other instruments that have beautiful shapes can be hung on walls or placed on shelves or tables to enhance the design of your gathering room.

A friend who plays the flute collected various types and sizes of flutes and displays them on a wall and shelf. She finds the patterns of musical notes on sheet music interesting and lively and frames copies of her favorite pieces, displaying them on a wall. I suggest that clients store recordings in wooden cabinets or put audiotapes in baskets, which will make choosing music a pleasurable experience.

A couple who enjoy dancing installed a hardwood floor where they can move about freely. To celebrate dancing they placed pictures and sculptures of dancers nearby.

A family I know uses games to honor the playful qualities of the soul. They put a game table in their gathering room near the fireplace and put a board game on it. Sometimes, they spread the pieces of a jigsaw puzzle on the table and put it together bit by bit over time. Another friend displays antique toys on shelves.

I enjoy going into people's homes and seeing their settings of meaningful photographs, objects, and mementos. A shelf or table with pictures of family, friends, places where they have lived and visited, and major events in their lives such as weddings and graduations tells the personal stories of their soul experience. A mother I know makes collages of images that capture the soul qualities of each individual in her household and displays them in the gathering room. She collects simple objects from events and travels that embody a world of meaning. She created a special shelf and table for displaying these memories. Another friend invites the artists he knows to display their work in his gathering room for a time.

REMODELING OR BUILDING A NEW GATHERING ROOM

When remodeling or building, consider the following ways of creating a soulful gathering room. If you are remodeling, observe the qualities of the present gathering room—shape and proportion; connection to adjacent rooms; size and placement of windows; qualities of light; and other features.

Begin the design of a remodeled gathering room or a new one by imagining gathering with family and friends in this room. Think of the conversations, stories, music, games, and other activities that will be enjoyed here. Imagine the holidays that will be celebrated here— Christmas, Hanukkah, birthdays. Think of the photographs, personal mementos, artwork, and other objects you would like to display in your gathering room and how you might exhibit them.

Envision the arrangement of seating and other furnishings that will best support the activities that will take place in your gathering room. Think of ways you might alter the existing room or shape the new one to support this soulful vision of gathering. A rectangular room could be designed to have focal points for various activities, such as a fireplace and seating at one end and a place for games or dancing at the other.

Think of the materials and colors that would give physical form to your vision of gathering. A fireplace of fieldstones would express rugged qualities of soul; a hearth with a marble surround and mantel

The design for an andiron recalls the solar fire that energizes the life of a home.

of carved cherry would express subtle nuances. Rugs and tapestries can soften the room, making it more cozy and intimate. Overscaled sofas with sumptuous cushions and soft fabrics in natural tones create a relaxed setting.

Find or design cabinets for displaying family photographs, stereo equipment, artwork, and other objects. Wooden cabinets with glass doors create a setting that honors the objects they contain. Install lighting that spotlights artwork, creating pools of light that augment more subdued lighting from lamps at the conversation areas.

My ideal gathering room is fifteen feet wide and twenty-five feet long. The ceiling rises to a central ridge that runs the length of the room. The ceiling of tongue-and-groove cedar is supported by a cedar ridge beam that rests on two large cedar trusses. The walls are plaster. The floor is two-and-one-quarter-inch hickory laid in a herringbone pattern. At one end of the room is a fireplace of honed limestone resting on a raised hearth. Its stone chimney rises to the peak of the roof where a skylight at the ridge admits moonlight. Spanning the opening of the firebox is a large, rough-hewn limestone lintel that contrasts with the regular pattern of the limestone courses on the rest of the fireplace. The walls framing the fireplace are lined with shelves that hold books, musical instruments, and stereo equipment. A special cabinet holds photographs of family and friends. In front of the fireplace, a semicircular sofa sits on a Persian carpet. The sofa is low to the floor with a seat of extra depth that invites cross-legged sitting. The cushions are plush, comfortable, and covered with a natural linen. At the other end of the room is a bay window with a built-in window seat. French doors and tall windows line one of the side walls. Lighting is provided by wall sconces.

7

Bedrooms

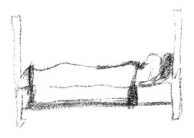

THE BEDROOM IS SHAPED BY THE PEACE OF SLEEP, THE FLIGHTS OF DREAM, AND THE CHARGED ENERGIES OF SEXUALITY. DESPITE ITS QUIET IMAGE, THE BEDROOM CONTAINS UNFATHOMABLE MYSTERIES AND POWER. THE BED IS THE SITE OF MANY OF OUR MOST INTIMATE AND MEANINGFUL EXPERIENCES. ARCHETYPALLY, IT CONTAINS THE TRANSFORMATIONS OF THE SOUL—THE AROUSAL AND SEXUAL COMMUNION THAT LED TO OUR CONCEPTION; THE ODYSSEY OF LABOR AND BIRTH; THE MOTHER'S VOICE, BABY BLANKET, AND CUDDLY TOY THAT GAVE US FIRST CONTACT WITH THE WORLD; THE FAIRY TALES AND MYTHIC STORIES THAT TAUGHT US CULTURAL VALUES; THE PASSAGES THROUGH CHILDHOOD ILLNESS; FIRST SEXUAL FANTASIES AND ROMANTIC ENCOUNTERS; THE NIGHTLY RENEWAL OF SLEEP; SECRET DREAMS AND INTIMATE LONGINGS; ADULT AGING AND ILLNESS; AND FINALLY THE PASSAGE ACROSS THE THRESHOLD OF DEATH. THE EMOTIONAL POWER OF THE BEDROOM MAKES IT FAR MORE THAN A COMFORTABLE PLACE TO REST OUR WEARY HEADS.

The softness and warmth of bedrooms coaxes us into tender regions of emotion. Sleep opens mind and body to innocence, simplicity, and security. Dreaming is a journey through wonder, surprise, and freedom. Sexuality animates passion, as well as vulnerability and poignancy.

SLEEPING AND DREAMING

The relationship of sleeping and dreaming to the soul has not been lost on poets and sages throughout time. "We are the stuff / As dreams are made of, and our little life / Is rounded with a sleep," wrote Shakespeare in *The Tempest.* This theme is echoed by the Bushmen of the Kalahari, who say that "there is a dream dreaming us." A continent away an Aztec poet wrote, "That we come to this earth to live is untrue: we come but to sleep, to dream."

"The dream," wrote Jung, "is a little hidden door into the innermost and most secret recesses of the soul." Joseph Campbell wrote in *The Mythic Image* that "the notion of this universe, its heavens, hells, and everything within it, [as] a great dream dreamed by a single being in which all the dream characters are dreaming, too, has in India enchanted and shaped an entire civilization." To embody this idea, the Indian god Vishnu, the

Dreams offer access to the treasures of the soul.

supporter and sustainer of the universe, is depicted floating on an ocean of milk while reclining on the coils of the abyssal serpent Ananta, whose name means "unending." Arising from Vishnu's navel is a lotus supporting Brahma, the Creator. Whenever Brahma opens his eyes, a universe is born; when he closes his eyes, a universe dissolves.

Resting gracefully on the sea, Vishnu is an archetypal image of the cradle, the cosmic ship of life on the primordial ocean. Associated with

A hand-carved wooden alcove and curtains create a warm niche that cradles a child's sleep and dreams.

the crescent of the new moon, the cradle embodies the sprouting of life and fresh beginnings. Cradles and beds are traditionally made of wood, which shelters us in the cribs of childhood to the caskets of death.

Bedrooms dwell in the nighttime realms, and our beds float on a lightless sea. Here are the realms of Hypnos, the Greek god of sleep, the son of Nyx (Night) and brother of Thanatos (Death). Hypnos lives in a dark and misty land. He dwells in a cavern by the river of forgetfulness and lies on a soft couch surrounded by an infinite number of sons, the Dreams. Leaving the daylight world and joining Hypnos in the bedroom, we reenter the primordial ground of being from which emerges the light of the soul. Bedrooms are therefore places of unmanifest light, of the dissolution of time, and of germination. Return from this nighttime world is sparked by the light of dawn, the sounding of the alarm clock, the step from the bed.

During dreaming and sleep, the limited possibilities of logical, waking consciousness give way to the mystical awareness of infinite possibilities. Flying over cities, talking to loved ones who have died, and other improbable experiences are the normal logic of dreamtime. Dreams convey messages from the soul to the conscious mind.

LOVEMAKING

A bottle of essential oils set on a windowsill connects a bedroom with lunar cycles.

Bedrooms are also the abodes of Eros and Psyche, the god and goddess of sensuous love and soul. Greek mythology describes how Psyche was so beautiful that people stopped worshiping her sister goddess Aphrodite. Aphrodite became so enraged that she ordered her son Eros to kill Psyche. When Eros (sensuous love) saw Psyche (soul), however, he fell in love with her. Eros devised a scheme whereby Psyche was taken by the wind to the safety of an enchanted palace with jeweled gates and golden floors. Psyche's needs were taken care of by unseen hands and a friendly voice. When she went to bed at night, Psyche was joined by Eros in human form. In the darkness he said, "I am your husband, and your life will be happy and full if only you

would refrain from seeking to find out who I am and how I look. If you do not obey, your children will be denied the immortality that is rightfully theirs."

Psyche fell deeply in love with Eros, but became lonely for her sisters. Reluctantly, Eros said he would fetch them, but warned Psyche not to listen to any questions about his identity. When Psyche's sisters saw her magnificent palace, they were filled with envy. When they learned that Psyche had never seen her husband, they frightened her, telling her that Eros would turn into a serpent that would crawl into her womb and devour her unborn baby.

Psyche went to bed that night overwhelmed with dread and curiosity. When Eros fell asleep, she took a lantern and a dagger. She lit the lamp and held it to Eros's face. Instead of a serpent, she saw the

Sun, moon, and stars link a cabinet to the rhythms of dusk and dawn.

Placing a bed by corner windows attunes sleeping, dreaming, and lovemaking to the cadence of sunrise and sunset.

beautiful features of the god of love and was so startled that a drop of oil fell from the lamp and landed on Eros's shoulder. Awakening to what Psyche had done, Eros rose into the air and flew away. Psyche surmounted the trials of separation by the help of earthly ants, growing reeds, and a heavenly eagle. She was deceived into a deathly sleep but was resurrected by the love of Eros. The spiritual love between Eros and Psyche overcame the jealous, material attachment of Aphrodite. The union of Eros and Psyche softened the hearts of the gods, who celebrated their marriage and bestowed upon them the nectar of immortality. "Where Eros stirs, Psyche is sure to be found," writes Phil Cousineau in *Soul: An Archaeology*. "Where Psyche performs her tasks, Eros draws near; when love nourishes soul, the soul is deepened through love. And no one touches the depths of the soul without love, the deepening god."

THE RHYTHMS OF NIGHT

Falling asleep and awakening in the bedroom recalls the waning and waxing rhythms of the moon, which influences the tides and the watery consciousness of slumber and dreams. The bedroom follows the cadence of sunset and sunrise, becoming a place of nightly hibernation and rebirth.

The bedroom immerses our senses in the subtle currents of the night. In darkness, our attention is drawn to the senses that integrate mind and body: hearing, touch, taste, and smell. Ears catch the subtle rustle of sheets, the creaks and groans of the bed, the sighs and brushes of love. Hands feel the smoothness of the linens and the electric curves of the skin. The mouth

Battenberg lace–edged curtains enfold a floral spread and pillows, inviting sleep and dreams.

savors the warm moistness of a kiss, while the nose is filled with the fragrances of hair and skin. Hormones stir into sexual urges as our bodies seek reproduction. On the bed our bodies recline, toss and turn, hug and stroke, rest and heal.

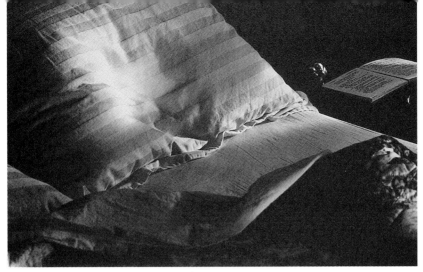

Layers of pattern and texture deepen a bed's soulfulness.

BEDS, LINENS, BLANKETS, AND FURNITURE

Eros and Psyche meet in the bed—the soft, level setting for reclining and relaxing. Here, mind and body can settle into the earthy urges of the soul. The word *bed* is used to denote places for sleeping, but also to describe areas for growing plants. The roots of the word carry the notion that a bed was originally a sleeping place dug into the ground like an animal's lair. Falling into sleep, all the muscles of the body can rest in the ground of their native state.

A rigid frame defines and contains the soft realm of the bed. It establishes a stable pedestal that honors sleeping, dreaming, and lovemaking by raising them above the floor. A four-poster frame further defines and enhances the sacredness of this space.

The mattress offers tender support. With loving-kindness it cushions us from the hardness of the world. Cloudlike, the mattress allows the soul to float in the sky of sleep and dreams.

Bed linens envelop the mattress, enhancing its softness. The particular weave and pattern of the sheets offers a field of nocturnal possibilities. Linen evokes luxurious sensuousness; cotton a cool freshness; flannel a cozy warmth; silk and satin can stimulate erotic fantasy. Flowered sheets can recall spring gardens or the rose-petal-strewn marriage beds of India. Images of superheros on children's sheets can wrap them in comfort and safety. Pillows rise to meet the head, creating downy supports for consciousness, inviting mental rest, dreaming, and imagination. Blankets tuck us into comfort and warmth; their cocooning embrace returns us to a womblike state. A down comforter reflects the cloudlike qualities of dreams.

A nightstand next to the bed serves our needs for the voyage into sleeping, dreaming, and loving. A book and a lamp to read by makes the transition from day to night. Sometimes we might place a candle there for romantic light, aroma oils for a more soothing rest, or a clock to alarm us into the day.

ARRANGING A SOULFUL BEDROOM

The soul qualities of a bedroom could be enhanced in the following ways. Use sheets and pillowcases that are sensuous to the touch, and change them to harmonize with the season—flannel in winter and cotton in summer. Also, vary the color according to the time of year—warm earth tones in autumn and winter, bright colors in spring, and pastels or whites in summer. Use

A restful place of simple elegance is created by an icon painting of an angel set above a carved wooden headboard with a rattan insert, and pillowcases with a lace insert and a tatting edge.

blankets with rich materials and colors, such as wool blankets of ethnic design, Amish quilts, or a down comforter. Vary these according to the season and your mood.

Drape a rich fabric or blanket over the headboard. String garlands of silk flowers over the headboard or along the bed frame. Hang a wreath or swag of dried flowers over the headboard.

On the nightstand by the bed, place a book of inspiring quotations, poetry, or stories. Place a beautiful journal and pen there and use them to record your dreams. Create space for using aromatic oils and candles.

Hang pictures of dream images on the walls.

REMODELING OR BUILDING A NEW BEDROOM

Begin the design of a remodeled or new bedroom by imagining going to sleep, awakening, and making love in this setting. Think of turning in at the end of the day on a summer's eve and a winter night, of rising at sunrise in the spring and in the dark of autumn. Visualize a romantic evening there.

A recessed alcove and shelves create a cozy setting for a bed.

Envision the bed and other furnishings that will best support the activities that will take place in your bedroom. Think of ways you might alter the existing room or shape the new one to support this soulful vision of sleeping, dreaming, and lovemaking. A square room provides an environment of balanced rest. A dormered ceiling offers cozy shelter.

Think of the materials and colors that would give physical form to your vision of gathering. A massive oak bed would encourage stability. A futon on a raised platform invites airy peace. A metal four-poster with diaphanous curtains stimulates fantasy. If you work with wood or know someone who does, build a bed frame that suggests the qualities of a boat or cradle floating on the waves. The headboard could be carved or painted with motifs that support the union of marriage with such symbols as the intertwining of male and female forms, the golden ring of wholeness, sun and moon, yin and yang, the king and queen, or the bridal symbols of boughs and branches. Buy a bed frame that has soft, sensuous lines such as a sleigh bed or an elegant

A bank of east-facing windows opens this bedroom to the sunrise.

four-poster. Hang luxurious fabric on the wall behind the bed or over the frame of a four-poster. Find bed linens and blankets with the textures and colors that you find restful.

Use wall sconces and other indirect lighting to create a soft glow of illumination. Put lighting on dimmer switches so you can vary the effect.

Paint or paper the walls with the colors and textures of evening and dawn. In a band running around the room at the top of the wall, paint depictions of the moon (in its waxing and waning phases), stars, and a sunrise (on the eastern wall). The deep hues of the night sky could tint the ceiling. The Renaissance philosopher Marcilio Ficino suggested that we paint the images of our astrological charts on the ceilings of our bedrooms. Paint or stencil the floor with flowing or sparkling patterns and watery colors to imply the ocean upon which we float in sleep and dream, or use a rug that has this theme.

My ideal bedroom is fourteen feet square. The peaked ceiling is painted a deep blue with stencils of the stars, the planets, and the moon. A cornice of cherrywood on two sides of the room, where the sloped ceiling meets the wall, provides indirect lighting on dimmer switches. A grouping of windows on the eastern wall forms a large arch. A Chinese wool carpet with a blue and green border depicting flowers and leaves rests on an oak floor. At the center of the room is an oak four-poster bed with an arched canopy. A lightweight, off-white cotton is draped over the arched frame and hangs to the floor. The fabric can be tied back to the posts to create an open feeling or pulled around the bed for cozy protection. The arched headboard is carved with a circle of flowering boughs and branches.

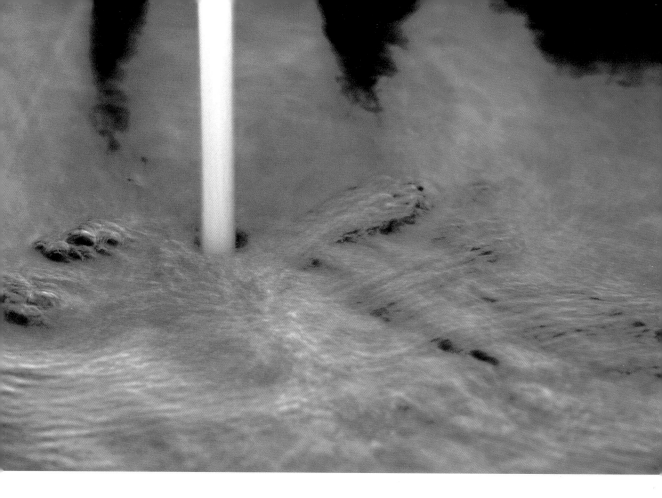

8

Bathrooms

THE WATERY CONSCIOUSNESS OF THE BEDROOM BECOMES THE WATERS OF PURIFICATION IN THE BATHROOM. WATER BUBBLING UP FROM UNSEEN DEPTHS WITHIN THE EARTH FLOWS INTO RESERVOIRS AND THROUGH UNDERGROUND PIPES TO BATHE AND REPLENISH. THE CONTRAST OF A FREE-FLOWING FLUID SPRINGING FROM UNMOVING, DENSE GROUND AND REVITALIZING THE EARTH EXPRESSES THE ARCHETYPAL MAGIC OF NATURE. THIS MAGIC IS BROUGHT TO THE SERVICE OF THE SOUL THROUGH THE DAILY RITUAL OF A MORNING SHOWER WHERE THE SLEEPINESS OF NIGHT SUBSIDES AND THE BODY IS INVIGORATED FOR THE DAY AHEAD.

Water's wondrous properties serve the practical needs of bathing and removing wastes while also linking material life to the depths of the soul. Life arises in water. Within the watery womb we grow from a tiny egg into our human form. Even though water has no nutritional value, all living creatures need a regular supply to fuel growth and change.

In mythic terms, the Water of the Spring, or Fountain of Life, rises around the roots of the Tree of Life in the center of paradise. Water, in the form of rain, represents the inseminating power of the sky god. Running water is perceived as being filled with vitality. Crossing a body of water is a symbol of the transformation from one state of consciousness to another. In Buddhist philosophy, traversing a body of water connotes the passage through illusion to enlightenment.

This notion becomes part of our daily experience during our morning routine when we pass through the waters of the bathroom, traveling from the illusions of dream to the light of day. Water that is below is equated with chaos, while water that comes from above signifies orderly, renewing powers. The bathroom expresses this archetypal theme in the toilet, which flushes waste down to the bowels of the house, and the shower, which rains hygiene and refreshment from above.

Animals that slither, wriggle, and dive embody the soul's watery qualities. Serpents, fish, frogs, whales, dolphins, crocodiles, and dragons evoke the undulating depths of unconsciousness.

The feminine qualities of soul are engaged through water. Aphrodite, goddess of love and the classic symbol of the feminine, emerged full grown from a foamy sea. Water's yielding nature is its strength. The Taoist philosophy of *wu-wei* describes this idea. Water readily yields when it reaches a point of resistance, enveloping the blocking form and passing beyond it, ultimately wearing down and dissolving it, even if it be the hardest rock. Thus, flexibil-

Stones and seashells in the corner of a shower recall mountain streams and oceans.

ity, as displayed by water, is a sign of life. Rigidity, its opposite, is an indicator of death.

Within the hard surfaces of the bathroom we, paradoxically, express the emotions of modesty, privacy, tenderness, openness, and intimacy. Sometimes harsher feelings of honesty and self-rejection appear under the glare of an unforgiving morning light, but these are usually softened by the misty air created by careful rituals of bathing

The bathroom is a paradox of textures. Smooth skin meets rough and hard brushes.

and brushing. The hard but smoothly curved surfaces of the tub, sink, and faucets invite the flow of water and the fluid gestures of hands, feet, and legs. Floor tiles and mirrors offer their cool, slick touch. Washing and massaging our bodies, we feel the soft smoothness of skin. Rough and hard-textured brushes cleanse hair and teeth, while rough and soft fibers of towels dry hair and skin.

The bathroom's qualities of light reflect similar sensory paradoxes. The sparkling surfaces of tile, porcelain, glass, and brass are softened by clouds of steaming water. As a child I used to marvel at how the piercing morning light of an east-facing bathroom window was softened by a galaxy of dust motes.

The flavors of the bathroom include toothpaste, mouthwash, and dental floss. The smells range from those of bodily waste and perspiration to scented soaps and perfumes.

BATHING

Bathing can mark a transition from night to day or from one stage of life to another. In ancient China, a bride and groom traditionally took a ceremonial bath before the wedding ceremony. Orthodox Jewish women take a ritual bath, a mikvah, seven days after the conclusion of monthly menstruation. Alchemists called the operation of dissolving

The purifying and revitalizing qualities of
water are made useful by the basin that
contains it.

a solution of sulfur and mercury the conjugal "bathing" of the king and queen; the soul was believed to be purified by the actions of washing, and the resulting spiritual transformation was signified by a shift in color from black to gray to white. In Buddhism, the ablutions that accompany the initiation of a monk represent the washing away of a layperson's past. Christianity sees bathing as a return to innocence; the lavabo, the washing of the priest's hands, signifies "I wash my hands in innocence." Islamic culture also considers bathing an important rite that returns humans to a state of primordial purity.

A specific assortment of actions accompanies bodily cleansing and renewal. The various rituals of scrubbing, lathering, dipping, massaging, brushing, drying, cutting, plucking, shaving, and painting with makeup and nail polish become so automatic that the skill of carrying them out is overlooked.

Bathing is essentially a means of restoring and maintaining physical and emotional health. Besides providing water for washing away impurities and replenishing the body's vitality, the bathroom contains medicines and instruments for treating disease and injury. The medicine cabinet holds an assortment of remedies, potions, and ointments as well as the odd collection of bandages, cotton swabs, and other devices for ministering to the body's ailments and disorders.

THE BODY

By caring for the body, the bathroom also cares for the soul. Each part of the body can be seen as a symbol of a different quality of soul. Hands, for example, represent strength and blessing.

Hands

Hands feed, dress, comfort, and build. Aristotle said that the "hand is the tool of tools." Think of all the objects in a home that allow our hands to express the impulses of the soul: doorknobs; handles of every sort—those found on cooking pots, faucets, and vacuum cleaners; buttons on telephones, television controls, and doorbells. Fingers portray the direction of power toward a given point. Fingers raised in benediction convey spiritual power.

Feet

Feet are symbols of freedom of movement and humility. Kissing or washing the feet indicates reverence. Footprints mark the path of transformation. The heel is the vulnerable part of the body that can also grind down evil.

Head

The head is the seat of intelligence and folly, signifying wisdom and the ability to rule. It is the object of both honor and dishonor with crowns of victory and ashes of penance. The face expresses the outward personality. The multiple faces depicted in statues and paintings of Hindu deities denote the different facets found within one personality.

Eyes

The eye is an emblem of omniscience, all-seeing divinity, and intuition. The eye's ability to see light is equated with the mind's ability to perceive the divine light of wisdom. In the West, the right eye is associated with the sun, and the left eye with the moon. In the East, these associations are reversed. "The light of the body is the eye," declares the Bible. Plato wrote, "There is an eye of the soul . . . by it alone Truth is seen." Freemasons placed the image of an all-seeing eye in a triangle and surrounded it with sunbeams as a symbol of the wisdom of the Creator, the Great Master Builder of All Worlds, who penetrates all secrets.

Mouth

The mouth depicts our emotions in frowns and smiles, openmouthed surprise, and tight-lipped fear. It receives nourishment and expresses ideas. Teeth are the most enduring part of the body and signify the determination to "bite through" circumstances.

Ears

The ear is associated with the spiral of creation, the whorls of seashells, and the sun. The ear is also a birth symbol linked to the vulva. The Indian god Karma, the son of the sun god, Surya, was said to have been born from his mother's ear. Christian art shows a dove, representing the Holy Ghost, entering the ear of the Virgin Mary prior to the Immaculate Conception.

Hair

Hair is the carrier of life force and conveys sensuality, sexuality, and virility. Hair on the head is related to the higher powers of inspiration; hair on the body is associated with lower animal powers. Hair flowing loose depicts freedom; bound, it represents control.

Belly

The belly in Western cultures represents the gross appetite. In the Orient, it is the seat of life and a symbol of prosperity. In alchemy, the darkness within the belly is the transforming laboratory, the labyrinth of transformation. The navel is a reflection of the cosmic center of creation.

Breasts

Breasts express nourishment and motherhood. Baring the breast is traditionally seen as a sign of humility, grief, repentance, or penitence.

Genitals

The vagina represents the womb of creation, the receptive and protective space within which matter is conceived and grows. In India, the linga (penis) combined with the yoni (vagina) signifies the unity of masculine and feminine forces that generate the physical world.

The penis expresses directed energy, potency, and fatherhood. Phallic symbols such as Hindu lingams and Egyptian obelisks represent the penetrating consciousness that stirs matter into living creation.

Blood

Blood is the symbol of life. In Christianity, one may commune with divinity through partaking of the blood and body of Christ. Bones stand for the indestructible life principle, the eternal essence of the soul that structures the universe. The heart is the seat of the soul, the dwelling place of God.

SINK, TUB, AND SHOWER

The fluid vitality of water is cupped and made useful by the various basins within the bathroom. The sink holds water in a raised basin for cleansing hands, face, and mouth. Tubs are lowered basins for immersing a sitting or reclining body. The elongated container of a shower stall wraps us in misty warmth.

A raised tub placed before a bank of windows provides a basin for immersing the body in water in a natural setting.

Basins containing water take on spiritual import for ritual purposes. Many spiritual practices begin with the washing of hands or the sprinkling of water to symbolize the cleansing of intention and the purging of worn-out thoughts and purposes. Soaking the body in water, as in bathing and baptism, symbolizes a return to the primordial state, a death to the old life and a rebirth into the new. It also represents the immersion of the soul in the manifest world. Dipping the

Sinks can become functional altars for honoring health and beauty. An apothecary cabinet that once held healing medicine makes a practical shrine for cleansing the body.

body in water represents delving into the ultimate mystery of life—how the formless energy of the universe gives rise to and shapes material form.

The sink honors the strength and blessing of the hands. The tub and shower tend to the whole body—readying the legs and feet to journey through the day; bathing the nourishing breast, the vital stomach, and supporting back; and awakening the intelligence and wisdom of the head.

TOILET

The toilet, despite its lowly status, is one of the most gracefully sculpted objects in a home. It receives the earthy by-products that pass through the labyrinth of the stomach. The toilet is the one place we actually stop for a moment of repose in a hectic day, making it a practical setting for contemplation. The theologian Martin Luther reported that he developed the ideas that led to the Protestant Reformation while sitting on the privy. The traditional Japanese toilet was likened to a meditation room by Jun'ichiro Tanizaki in his book *In Praise of Shadows:*

The parlor may have its charms, but the Japanese toilet is truly a place of spiritual repose. . . . No words can describe that sensation as one sits in the dim light, basking in the faint glow reflected in the shoji, lost in meditation or gazing out at the garden. . . . I love to listen from such a toilet to the sound of softly falling rain. . . . And the toilet is the perfect place to listen to the chirping of insects or the song of birds, to view the moon, or to enjoy the poignant moments that mark the change of the seasons. Here, I suspect, is the place where haiku poets over the ages have come by a great many of their ideas. . . . Our forebears, making poetry of everything in their lives, transformed what by rights should be the most unsanitary room in the house into a place of unsurpassed elegance, replete with fond associations with the beauties of nature.

MIRROR

Gazing into the mirror, we see how the soul is expressed in our outward personality. We look directly into the soul through the "windows" of our eyes and perceive the shape of our emotions in the attitude of our mouth.

The mirror signifies truth, self-knowledge, wisdom, the mind, and the soul. Chuang Tzu said, "The mind of the sage, being in repose, becomes the mirror of the universe." Being too caught up in a mirror's reflection recalls the fate of Narcissus, the youth so enamored of the reflection of his own beauty in a pool of water that the more he looked the deeper he fell in love with himself. Day after day he lay beside the pool entranced, until finally he wasted away and died.

The eye of wisdom placed over the Masonic symbols of the compass and the mason's square reminds those who use this bathroom that the mirror signifies the truth, self-knowledge, and wisdom of the soul.

Combing our hair in the mirror, we touch our strength and sexuality. The comb is an attribute of Venus. It signifies fertility and the removal of entanglement. The teeth of a comb represent rain and rays of the sun. Combs are symbols of music and the mythic Sirens of Greece, whose prophetic songs were so enchanting that passing sailors were compelled to stop and listen forever. A "bad hair day" has implications that go beyond a lifeless hairstyle.

ARRANGING A SOULFUL BATHROOM

I suggest enhancing the design of the bathroom in a number of ways. At the sink use seashells or smooth river stones to hold soap, razors, brushes. Around the tub and shower, place displays of seashells and river rocks or stones. Use them to hold natural sponges and soaps.

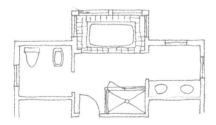

A wicker hamper adds airy texture to a bathroom.

Hang a body brush with a wooden handle from the wall. Store bath oils around the tub in baskets or on special shelves.

Put a wooden seat on the toilet. Make a little shelf near the toilet where you can place a picture of a beautiful view, an interesting object, or a poem to contemplate. Change the object you put on this shelf occasionally to reflect the season or your mood.

Surround the mirror with garlands of dried flowers or pine boughs. Find a picture frame that inspires you, put a mirror in it, and use it as your bathroom mirror.

Find an old cabinet with glass doors and use it as a medicine cabinet. Buy luxurious towels and bathrobes. Store towels in baskets or wooden bins.

On the walls, hang pictures that honor the grace and beauty of the body. Use photographs and paintings of waterfalls, rivers, and lakes, and water creatures such as fish, dolphins, mermaids, sea horses, and starfish. Make the bathroom feel more like a natural setting by using patterns of wallpaper and colors of paint that recall a forest's layered hues. Place a luxurious bath mat or rug on the floor.

Introduce plants wherever possible. If the sunlight is inadequate, grow lights can be installed.

REMODELING OR BUILDING A NEW BATHROOM

When remodeling or building, consider the following ways of creating a soulful bathroom. If you are remodeling, observe the qualities of the present bathroom—shape and proportion; connection to adjacent rooms; size and placement of windows; qualities of light; and other features.

Begin the design of a remodeled bathroom or a new one by imagining bathing in this room. Think of your morning ritual of brushing teeth, showering, using the toilet, and grooming. Imagine times when you might relax by soaking in a warm tub. Envision the arrangement of tub, shower, toilet, lavatory, mirror(s), medicine cabinet, towel bars, robe hooks, and other elements that will best support your vision of bathing and grooming. Think of ways you might alter the existing room or shape the new one to support this soulful vision of bathing.

A pedestal sink focuses attention on the daily rite of washing your hands, face, and mouth. A vanity cabinet made of oak or other wood with a countertop of marble or granite adds naturalness and texture. A wide showerhead creates a rain of water. A bay window or deepened windowsill by the tub can hold a small, sunny garden of houseplants to bathe beside. Situating the toilet by a window provides a view to contemplate.

Think of the materials and colors that would give physical form to your vision of bathing. Ceramic tiles with watery colors, such as blues and greens, recall streams, lakes, and vegetation; earth tones recall rocks and sand. Arrange the tiles in lively or random patterns that imitate a play of water. On the floor, install oak, teak, or other hardwood instead of tile. Use limestone or marble on the floor installed with in-floor heating.

Soften the hardness of the bathroom by subduing the quality of light with the use of dimmer switches and/or candles. Use an inset soap dish by the tub to hold candles. Put task lighting where you need it, at the mirror and in other spots, for the practical functions of applying makeup and grooming.

My ideal bathroom is fifteen feet wide by twelve feet deep. It has a plaster barrel-vaulted ceiling that rests on plaster walls. A wainscot of one-and-a-half-inch-wide tongue-and-groove teak rises thirty inches. The floor is made of a twenty-four-inch-by-twenty-four-inch grid of three-inch-wide teak strips that frame mosaics of two-inch-by-two-inch granite and limestone tiles placed in a shimmering checkerboard pattern. At the center of one of the long walls is a rectangular bay window that frames a large clawfoot tub. Tall windows in deep frames fill out the three sides of the bay. On either side of the bay-window tub is a pedestal sink. Above each sink is a ledge with small cabinets for toothbrushes, razors, and other personal items. Over each sink and cabinet is a round mirror flanked by two small wall sconces. To the side of each sink is a small window that receives daylight. At the center of the opposite wall is the shower. The back wall of the shower is rough-hewn granite with shelves for holding plants that thrive on steamy water. The other three sides of the shower enclosure, including the shower door, are one-half-inch-thick tempered glass. To the left of the shower enclosure is the toilet. To the right is a teak cabinet that holds towels, soaps, bath oils, and other bathroom paraphernalia.

9

Clothes Closets

"In every fashion, in every form of dress, the Architectural Idea is ever-present. The body and the suit represent the place and the material on which—and with which—one must construct the splendid edifice of the personality."

Thomas Carlyle

A clothes closet is a chapel for dressing. Far-fetched as this may seem, the word *chapel* has a very specific source. It was originally applied to the shrine built to preserve the cloak of Saint Martin of Tours as a holy relic. Articles of clothing in a closet are like holy relics; they remind us of the indwelling powers of the soul. A business suit reminds us to express the spirit of orderliness, focused attention, and achievement. A Hawaiian shirt holds the attitude of a warm trade wind.

Closets, armoires, dressers, and other containers of clothing are like the sacred arks that contain secret wisdom about our personalities. Each article of clothing within them reveals the particular ways that soul is expressed in our individuality, the images of appearance that are personally significant. The power tie, the sweater knitted by a relative, the shoes designed to walk the varied terrain of a week, and other items display intimate links with our deepest selves. Drawers for personal items are cousins to the sacred arks that hold obscure wisdom to which outsiders have no access.

From our closet/arks we withdraw the clothing that both veils and reveals the soul. In the sacred teachings of many cultures, the body is likened to an article of clothing worn by the soul. The Bhagavad Gita, for example, conveys this notion by stating, "As a man casting off worn-out garments takes other new ones, so the dweller in the body casting off worn-out bodies takes on others that are new." In a lifetime, the core of our personality, our soul, witnesses

Mahogany cabinets honor the act of dressing by providing custom-designed shelves, drawers, and closets to receive each article of clothing.

the casting off of several worn-out bodies for new ones. Our childhood body is exchanged for the body of adolescence; the body of youth is discarded for the body of midlife and old age. In the course of a day, our souls can witness the casting off of one garment in exchange for others—pajamas give way to outfits for exercise, work, social occasions, and relaxing around the house.

Clothing acts like a mask that gives the wearer the power to stand out or to blend in with surroundings. Choosing a shirt or blouse from a closet, we select a mask that allows us to harmonize or contrast with those around us. Masks in sacred plays display the hidden forces of the soul. In secular plays, they reveal the inner characteristics that may normally be concealed by the outward personality. Closets are the backstage areas where we don the masks that will show the forces of soul and character hidden within us.

Above **Paintings of Adam and Eve wearing fig leaves bring a humorous twist to the mythic images of dressing.**

Opposite **A pediment atop an armoire creates a sacred cabinet for storing shirts and sweaters.**

The type of mask we select reestablishes communion with the specific energies portrayed by that form. A pair of hiking boots, whether they are worn on a mountain trail or a Manhattan sidewalk, reconnect us with nature's rugged earthiness. Depending on our mood, we can use our closets as places to reestablish our links with the muses of abundance, good cheer, diligence, and other qualities of the soul.

CLOTHING

Layers of clothing enrich the concealing and revealing qualities of the masks we wear. The three layers of apparel—undergarments, outerwear, and overcoats—can be related to the three layers of our personality—inner soul essence, outer personality, and the environment that affects us. Closets are often arranged in sections that acknowledge these layers.

The material and cut of our clothing have an emotional impact. Soft, flowing robes encourage graceful, fluid movement. Precisely tailored jackets and pants urge strict formality. Richly textured woolens convey warmth in contrast to the coolness of smooth silks. Color and pattern add other layers of meaning.

Clothing links us to the cycles of nature. We respond to the warmth of the sun, the coolness of the wind and rain, the time of day, and the season of the year by wearing clothing that is appropriate.

Sportswear, work clothes, casual clothes, bedclothes, and other attire are precisely designed to connect mind, body, and action.

Coats, shoes, hats, belts, and other items are of particular symbolic importance.

Clothing reveals personal expressions of soul.

Coats

Coats are capable of sheltering the entire body. They can bring visual unity to our appearance, conveying the image of consolidated energy and power. Because of this effect, coronation robes are part of the finery of rulers. Various Christian saints, such as Francis of Paola, are said to have crossed over water with the help of their capes. Saint Francis of Assisi divided his cape with beggars, symbolically sharing his power. Capes and cloaks are also symbols of protective enclosure. Raincoats, parkas, windbreakers, and other jackets translate this idea into practical reality. Wrapping one's own coat around another is an act of loving-kindness.

Shoes

Shoes signify freedom, authority, and humility. They give us freedom to walk without pain or injury and the liberty to roam the earth. Removing shoes at the entry to a holy place is a practical act of leaving the dust and the dirt of the road outside. It is also symbolic of leaving behind the outward pull of worldly obligations to enter the inward peace of the sacred. One of the most effective and easy ways of cultivating a feeling of sacredness in a home is to remove your shoes when entering. Leaving shoes at the door, we slip out of the worldly persona of the day and step into our unadorned, essential nature.

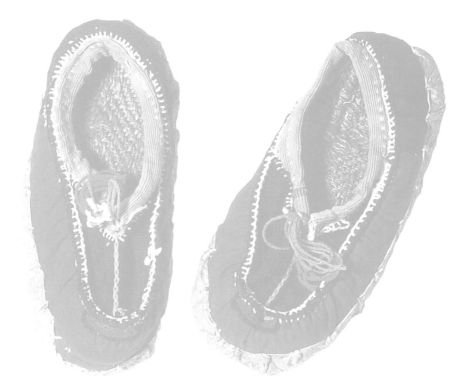

Different styles of shoes express varied characters of the soul. By choosing sensible pumps, sexy heels, traditional loafers, sober wing tips, energetic sneakers, or other fashions, we express these traits of the spirit on the pathways of our daily activities.

Hats

Hats also express personality. Since we see them worn near eye level, they are usually the first item of clothing we notice. By making the wearer appear taller, hats convey power and authority. Whereas shoes are shaped in relation to the earth they touch, hats are formed in relation to the sky. A baseball cap shades the eyes from the sun. Other hats protect from rain and wind. In this way hats mark changes in the seasons. Resting on the head, hats represent our state of mind. Changing hats equals a change in attitude. Hats can indicate social status. Caps have become billboards for advertising products, causes, and places.

Belts

Belts and sashes encircle the body, offering a feeling of safety. They visually divide the body, reflecting the junction of our skyward and earthy natures. Belt buckles celebrate this juncture by being adorned with symbols. *Girdle* is another name for belt; Homer called the Milky Way the "Girdle of Aphrodite" to symbolize love encircling all. Various types of belts, such as chastity belts, have been associated with the confinement or enclosure of sexuality. In former times, the removal of the bridal sash on the wedding night signified the consummation of the marriage. In Persia, a cord passed three times around the waist served as a reminder of the virtues of good thoughts, good words, good actions.

> Layers of clothing recall three aspects of the soul—inner essence, outer persona, and cultural surroundings.

Jewelry

Jewelry embodies the soul's wealth.

Jewelry symbolizes hidden treasures of knowledge or truth and a display of inner wealth. The cutting and shaping of gems signifies the individual soul that is shaped from the rough, irregular, dark stone of the universal soul. The regular shape of gems signifies how orderliness can reflect divine light within the chaos of the world. "The jewel is in the lotus of the world," declares the Buddhist sutra *Om mani padme hum*.

Gems and metals have been linked since ancient times to the astrology of planets and stars. In the Vedic system of astrology called *jyotish*, it is believed that wearing the gem ruled by a particular planet strengthens the influence of that planet in an individual's life. Wearing pearls, for example, is said to strengthen the moods and mental happiness influenced by the moon. Diamonds are said to enhance the love and beauty associated with the planet Venus. In this sense, jewelry boxes contain a universe of symbolic power. Each gem and metal reveals another star in the constellation of the soul.

A silver case for eyeglasses honors seeing.

Gold

Gold is linked to the sun. It represents inner and outer illumination, sacredness, incorruptibility, wisdom, durability, nobility, honor, wealth, and superiority. In alchemy, gold signifies attainment of the center, the goal, the heart, perfection, wholeness, and congealed light. Gold is said to strengthen the soul, vitality, self-reliance, professional status, the eyes, and the heart. Rubies are also associated with the sun. They express royalty, dignity, zeal, power, love, passion, beauty, longevity, and invulnerability.

Diamonds

Diamonds, associated with Venus, are symbolic of light, life, durability, invincibility, constancy, sincerity, and innocence. Diamonds are said to strengthen matters of romance, comfort, prosperity, happiness, beauty, sensuality, artistic pursuits, and the reproductive system.

Emeralds

Emeralds are connected to the planet Mercury. They signify immortality, hope, spring, youth, and faithfulness. Emeralds are said to enhance intelligence, poetic speech, confidence, communication, writing, drawing, commerce and trade, humor and wit, the nervous system, lungs, and intestines.

Pearls and Silver

Pearls and silver, linked to the moon, denote the feminine principle, the waters, chastity, and purity. Pearls and silver are said to strengthen memory, common sense, emotional stability, general well-being, romance, the feminine, the breasts, and the brain.

Coral

Red coral is associated with Mars. Greek mythology describes coral as originating from the severed head of the Gorgon Medusa when the drops of her blood touched the sand. Coral is said to strengthen courage, technical ability, leadership, motivation, physical prowess, and passion.

Topaz and Sapphire

Topaz is linked to Jupiter. It signifies divine goodness, faithfulness, friendship, love, and insight. Topaz is said to strengthen prosperity, luck, opportunity, spirituality, wisdom, compassion, the liver, resistance to allergies, and the thighs.

The blue sapphire is associated with Saturn and expresses truth, heavenly virtues, and celestial contemplation. It is said to strengthen longevity, discipline, leadership, wisdom born of experience, organization, teeth, and bones.

ARRANGING, REMODELING, OR
BUILDING A NEW CLOTHES CLOSET

Remove all clothing that you aren't excited about or haven't worn in the past year. Arrange skirts, blouses, pants, shirts, and other articles of clothing according to color or fabric and texture.

When remodeling or building, consider the following ways of creating a soulful clothes closet. If you are remodeling, observe the qualities of the present closet—shape and proportion; connection to adjacent rooms; size and placement of windows; qualities of light; and other features.

Begin the design of a remodeled closet or a new one by imagining your morning routine of choosing and putting on clothing. Imagine the different activities and occasions you dress for, such as work, exercise, and social events. Envision how you dress for the different seasons. Think of ways you might alter the existing closet or shape the new one to support this soulful vision of dressing. If you are building a new house, consider designing a clothes closet you can dress in.

Buy wooden or plastic clothes hangers and/or install beautiful brass clothes hooks. Install shoe racks or hanging shoe pockets. Store folded clothing in wooden cabinets with glass doors. Store hats and gloves in baskets. Buy an armoire or dresser made of rich hardwoods or find old ones and paint them in rich colors. Buy or make a clothes chest of aromatic cedar. Buy an interesting jewelry box. Display necklaces, bracelets, and earrings on hooks. Install a full-length mirror and side lighting that enhances your appearance.

My ideal is a walk-in clothes closet measuring nine feet wide by eight feet long. Double-high oak clothes poles with wooden hangers line one wall. The opposite wall is lined with oak drawers with glass doors and oak shelves. A skylight floods the room with light. A full-length mirror with an elegant oak frame flanked by wall sconces hangs at one end of the room.

10

Home Offices

Handling money and doing accounts play an essential role in a home for the soul. The roots of the word *economy* mean "household management" — from the Greek *oikos* (house) and *nemein* (manage). Since ancient times, women in India have endeavored to enhance the connection between home and money.

Each day women in many parts of India paint sacred designs at the doorways as an invitation to Lakshmi, the goddess of wealth and abundance. In our homes, the task of paying bills and keeping track of finances may seem like a depressing necessity, but understanding the deeper nature of home finance can transform it into a soulful endeavor.

In India, sacred diagrams are placed at entries as invitations to the goddess of wealth.

From the material point of view, money is the most powerful influence in a home. We say that money puts a roof over our heads and food on the table. Think of how much of your day is spent making money, spending it, wanting it, worrying about it, and counting it. Most of the money we earn goes in some way toward supporting our homes.

Money, considered the most materialistic of substances, expresses many attributes of the soul. Like the soul, money can be used to influence the material surroundings. Money, having no substance itself, can buy shelter from wind, rain, and sun. It purchases furniture, clothing, heat for warmth and cooking, light for illumination, books for inspiration, and innumerable other possessions and services.

In fairy tales, gold is often used as a symbol of spiritual power and realization. Straw is spun into gold, geese lay golden eggs, gold coins are magically produced from the pocket of a cloak. In the Grimm Brothers' story "The Star Money," a young girl is left without home and family, with only the clothes she wears and a bit of food. The girl travels through the countryside and meets many unfortunate people. One by one she gives them her food, her hood, her jacket, and dress. At last, on a dark night in a forest, she gives away her last possession, her shirt. "And," the story goes, "as she so stood, and had not a single thing left, suddenly some stars from heaven fell down, and they were nothing else than hard, smooth pieces of money, and although she had just given her shirt away, she had a new one that was of the finest linen. Then she put the new money into it and was rich all the days of her life."

Mythological treasures also play a role in the spiritual understanding of money. Commonly portrayed as hidden in caves or underground, treasures in folklore are found by passing through trials and overcoming demons. The search is usually assisted by supernatural power and leads to the discovery of one's true spiritual nature. A story from Eastern Europe expresses this theme. A man had a dream that a treasure of gold coins was buried under a bridge in Prague. The man followed the prompting of his dream and traveled many days until he reached the city. To his great joy he found the bridge he had seen in his sleep, but it was guarded by a soldier. For several days he visited the bridge, deterred each time by the sentry who stood watch. The soldier noticed this man and asked him what he was doing, and the man told the story of his dream. The two agreed that they would dig for the trove together, but after much backbreaking work, they found nothing. When they had given up, the soldier said, "You know, it's odd, but I had a dream the other night about a house with a sack of gold hidden under the floorboards behind the stove." As the soldier described the details of the dream, the man recognized the vision as his own house. He returned home to find his treasure hidden behind the stove.

Numbers

Money in its various forms has always been measured through the use of numbers. Since ancient times, numbers have been considered primal symbols of spirit in material form. Numbers are seen as the organizing principle that produces the underlying harmony of the universe. Pythagoras said that "everything is disposed according to numbers." Aristotle wrote that number was "the origin and, as it were, the substance of all things."

Zero represents unmanifest, limitless potential, the ultimate mystery. It is the source and receptacle of the physical universe, the cosmic egg. In its circular form, zero depicts death and the possibility of new life. As an oval, it signifies the rise and fall of awakened consciousness.

One is the first stirring of soul into manifestation. It is unity, the vital essence, the center of the cosmos. One is the force that gives rise to the diversity of creation. One is God, the Creator, and the hidden intelligence within all things. It is the experience of "I am, I exist." One is the geometric figure of the point.

Two is duality, diversity, and dependence. Alchemists used the number two to represent the opposites of sun and moon or king and queen. It depicted the conflict that resolves into unity. Two is the line connecting two points.

Three is multiplicity, creative power, and growth. The Vedas describe three forces of nature, the *gunas*, that create, maintain, and dissolve the physical world. All cultures use three to depict the principles of beginning-middle-end, past-present-future, heaven-man-earth.

The needs and dreams of the psyche are revealed through the management of home finances.

The plots in many myths, legends, and stories revolve around the number three: three wishes, three attempts at reaching a goal, three sisters, for example. Many religions use a trinity of deities or powers such as the Father, Son, and Holy Spirit of Christianity or Brahma, Vishnu, and Shiva of Hinduism. Buddhism has the Three Jewels of the Buddha (the teacher), the Dharma (the knowledge), and the Sangha (the spiritual community). The triangle forms the geometry of three. It is also represented by the trident and the fleur-de-lis.

Four is manifest wholeness and totality. It is the all-encompassing space and time of the four directions and the four seasons. Four is the number of the earth. It is depicted by the square and the cross.

Five is the microcosm within the human body. It is the number of human form and experience—the head with arms and legs, the five fingers on each hand, toes on each foot, and the five senses. Five takes the geometric form of the star and the pentagon.

Six is the symbol of equilibrium and harmony. In the form of two interlaced triangles, six signifies the union of male and female, heaven and earth, fire and water. It therefore represents love, health, and beauty. Six is depicted by the hexagon and the six-pointed star or the seal of Solomon.

Seven represents the macrocosm, the totality of the universe. It integrates spirit and matter by combining the three of the heavens and the soul with the four of the earth and the body. Seven is the number of days in the week, notes in a musical scale, colors in the rainbow, major planets, and heavens and hells. It is said to be the number of perfection, security, reintegration, and the Great Mother.

Eight is the number of paradise, the spiritual goal of passing through seven stages of spiritual experience. As the sum of seven plus one, eight is the symbol of regeneration. Its geometric form is the octagon.

Nine, being the sum of three times three or the Trinity times the Trinity, is considered a symbol of spiritual completeness and fulfillment. A grid of nine squares, three by three, has been used as  the guiding principle in architectural floor plans for thousands of years. Almost all of the houses designed by the Renaissance architect Andrea Palladio used a planning grid of nine squares.

Ten is the cosmic number. It is a symbol of creation. Being the sum of one plus two plus three plus four, ten is all-inclusive of time and space: one is a point; two, a line; three, a plane; four, space. The ten fingers of the two hands are the basis of our counting system. The Chinese phrase *the ten thousand things* denotes the innumerable forms of physical manifestation, the totality of creation. The Rig Veda describes the whole of the physical universe in ten mandalas, or cycles, of verse. The Hebrew Cabala describes ten as the number of yod, the Eternal Word and first letter of the name of God. Ten is the number of returning to the source. Odysseus journeyed for nine years and arrived home on the tenth.

Money is usually counted using a pen or pencil (calculators and computers are high-tech pens). In Egypt, the pen was seen as symbolizing the awakening of the soul. In Islamic countries, it signifies universal intelligence, the Spirit, that inscribes the story of life on the tablet of the unmanifest. A pen is a tool of infinite potential. It holds unlimited possibilities for revealing the patterns and expressions of the soul.

A walnut secretary by a window seat creates a light-filled setting for corresponding with friends and paying bills.

WORKING AT HOME

The place where we account for money can also be a setting for creating it. With the current trend toward corporate downsizing and the "have skill, will travel" approach to work, home offices are growing in

Above **A primitive mask reconnects an office to the energies of ancient ritual.**

Right **The elegant lines of this wood and leather chair transform a functional office into a setting for artful business.**

A photographer uses a bay-windowed room as a luminous office.

importance. Working at home also provides the opportunity to conduct business in styles that are more personal and soulful. We can work at a pace that responds to our individual needs in environments that delight and inspire us.

Even though we don't usually consider it in this way, work is a means of expressing the spirit. Through work, we offer particular qualities of soul in exchange for compensation. An architect offers the consciousness of organization and design. A psychologist serves patients with the consciousness of listening and responsive advice. A cabinetmaker gives clients the consciousness of shaping, joining, and finishing wood for useful purposes.

A setting that encourages soulful work honors the particular qualities of consciousness that a person offers through his or her vocation. Furniture, equipment, qualities of light, color, texture, space, artwork, and time are the elements that can be used to create a place for working that is receptive to soul.

ARRANGING A SOULFUL HOME OFFICE

Set aside an area for managing home finance. A simple table, filing cabinet, and bookshelf will do. Make this area a place for honoring the soulful aspects of wealth and abundance. Display images such as a

An executive placed this vase on the windowsill of his office as a reminder to work with vitality and joy.

fertile earth goddess, Juno, or Lakshmi, the Vedic goddess of wealth. Hang pictures of fertile fields and orchards and abundant harvests. Place coins in a basket or wooden bowl.

Depict the organizing power of numbers by using geometric designs on wallpaper, a rug, or framed prints. On the desk, use cubes, pyramids, and other geometrically shaped objects for paperweights.

Hang photographs that honor your activities which create

wealth and abundance. Buy stationery that has substance and texture. Purchase a high-quality address book that honors the people and businesses that are recorded in it. Use wooden or stone bowls, baskets, or interesting boxes to store paper clips, stamps, and other supplies.

REMODELING OR BUILDING A NEW HOME OFFICE

When remodeling or building, consider the following ways of creating a soulful home office. If you are remodeling, observe the qualities of the present room—shape and proportion; connection to adjacent rooms; size and placement of windows; qualities of light; and other features.

Begin the design of a remodeled home office or a new one by imagining working in this room. Think of the way you pay bills and taxes and keep your financial records. Imagine creative work you would like to do in your home office. Envision the arrangement of desk, computer, files, fax machine, bookshelves, worktables, lamps, and other equipment that will best support your vision of soulful work. Think of ways you might alter the existing room or shape the new one to create a home office with soul.

Think of the materials and colors that you associate with soulful work. Oak imparts strength and stability. An ergonomically designed chair provides comfort and alertness. Large windows invite expansive vision. Provide task lighting where you need it.

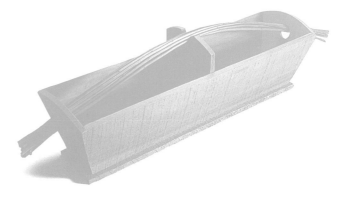

My ideal home office is a room twelve feet wide by fifteen feet long. The ceiling, which rises to a peak, is supported by maple beams. At one end of the room, French doors surrounded by windows open to a courtyard garden. On the other side of the room is a built-in U-shaped desk of maple; part of the desk is for drafting, another part holds a computer for writing. Over the central part of the U is a window. Maple bookshelves atop maple lateral files line the remainder of the side walls of the room. In the open space near the French doors, a wool rug rests on the maple floor. A small sofa and a comfortable chair sit on the rug.

II

Places of Solitude

THE DYNAMIC ACTIVITIES OF A HOME ARE NOURISHED BY TIMES AND PLACES OF QUIET AND SOLITUDE. SOLITUDE ALLOWS US TO TOUCH THE DEPTHS OF THE SOUL. IN THE RESTFUL ALERTNESS OF MEDITATION, PRAYER, STUDY, WRITING, DRAWING, AND PLAYING MUSIC, THE MIND AND BODY SETTLE INTO THE LUMINOUS SILENCE OF OUR TRUE NATURE. DURING THE ACTIVE SOLITUDE ENCOUNTERED IN EXERCISE, YOGA, OR TAI CHI, WE LEARN TO INTEGRATE THE SILENCE OF THE SOUL WITH DYNAMIC MOVEMENT.

Creating a setting in order to let go of demands and obligations literally "gives us space" to regain our center and be replenished by the depths of the soul. A place of solitude offers a retreat from the opposing forces and diverse demands of living, an entry into a state of peace and unity. Mind and body can retire from confusion and conflict to a sanctuary of clarity and harmony. The wear and tear of time can give way to the healing renewal of timelessness. We can step out of the details that command our attention and regain the broader freedom of the big picture.

A place of solitude provides a setting for rediscovering the dormant powers within us. In the silence of such a place we can listen to the soul whispering its needs and dreams. The noisy static created by

An attic dormer is transformed into a quiet meditation retreat. The cathedral-shaped window, lowered altar, and pillows add an air of sacredness.

the constant chatter of activity subsides and the wisdom of the spirit can be heard. In a setting created for solitary pursuits, the heart and mind can open to the silent depths of the soul.

Places conducive to solitude are stable and orderly. Sounds are muted and draw the mind toward quietness. Textures are soft and smooth. Light and colors are quiet and harmonious. Fragrances are soothing and fresh. Seating is comfortable but encourages alertness; it might be low to the floor.

ALTARS

An altar, niche, or table in a place of solitude can focus attention on objects and emblems that expand and

A window seat creates a quiet alcove for contemplation.

deepen soul experience. The original meaning of the word *altar* is a place of sacrificial burning. Altars in this sense are places for symbolically burning away the emotional hurt, anger, and frustration that

accumulate in daily life. Sacred diagrams, images, and icons can transport the mind from the harsh, discordant levels of life to inner realms of subtlety and oneness. Candles can radiate a quiet, golden light that is conducive to the inward turn of consciousness. Incense spreads fragrance that urges peacefulness.

Traditionally, altars have been places for experiencing the presence of the divine. They are thresholds for reuniting with the lost powers of the soul and integrating them into thought and action. Altars are places for expressing gratitude, for appreciating the gifts that life has brought. Addressing an altar placed on the east side of a room allows one to face the direction of the rising sun, honor the forces that regenerate life, and allow one's thoughts to flow in the symbolic direction of paradise. Raised altars imply a ritual ascent. An altar at floor level draws attention toward groundedness and integration.

The materials used to create an altar convey additional meaning. Stone signifies timelessness and the immortal nature of the soul. Wood implies the manifestations of the soul's growth and transformation through time. Covering a table used for an altar with cloth can symbolize the interconnected fabric of existence.

A simple window can become an altar for contemplating the ways that the soul shapes the physical world. It creates a fixed frame for viewing the constant changes in the material environment. We may consider the material environment a collection of static objects, but it is in constant flux. Sunlight washes over a tree or a building at different times of the day and year, changing the colors and shadows. People come and go. Rain, snow, clouds, and sunshine affect the scene. The sill of a window that overlooks this

Above **Natural objects and a handcrafted bowl make an altar for contemplating the beauty of creation.**

Opposite **Blankets, pillows, and a personal object are used to turn the corner of a room into a place for meditation.**

fluid scene can be used as a narrow altar for honoring objects that catch the sunlight, reminding us of the luminous nature of the spirit.

BOOKS

Books are like small altars, each page serving as a threshold for crossing into realms of broadened vision. As containers of insight and understanding, books play a vital role in gaining spiritual wisdom. The Jewish mystics of the thirteenth century wrote in the *Sepher Razielisthat* that when the angel Rasiel appeared to Adam, he said, "I have come to give insight into pure teachings and great wisdom, to make you familiar with the words of this holy book." Christian symbolism portrays the absorbing of wisdom with the image of the prophet John swallowing the Book of Revelation. An open book depicts the knowledge that one gains on the path of spiritual awakening. A book and pen signify the interaction of spirit and matter—the book is the emblem of matter and the pen symbolizes the dynamic power and creativity of the spirit.

SILENCE AND RENEWAL

Soulfulness is deepened by taking a few moments each day to enter the silence and renewal of your place of solitude, meditating or listening to music that quiets your mind and body. The altar can be used to contemplate objects and pictures that inspire you with wisdom and compassion. A few lines read from a book provide a focus for insight and understanding.

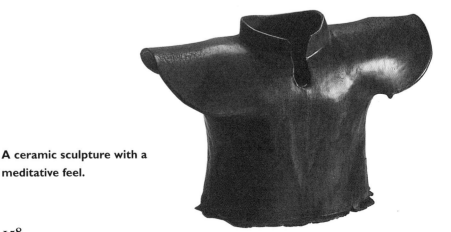

A ceramic sculpture with a meditative feel.

ARRANGING A PLACE OF SOLITUDE

Set aside a room, a closet, or the corner of a room as a place of solitude. Mark this space with an altar, a special chair, or other seating. Create a focus of attention by arranging the seating so it faces a window with an inspiring view, a picture of a peaceful setting, or an object that invites contemplation.

Drape cloth over a table or shelf and place objects on it that give you a sense of the sacred: pictures or statues of deities, angels, or spiritual teachers; stones, leaves, seashells, fruit, or flowers; bells, candles, and incense. Open a book to an inspiring quote or photograph and place it on this table or shelf. Changing the objects with the season can assist you in exploring various themes of solitude. Create an altar using these objects inside a cabinet.

In your place of solitude, create a setting that honors reading with a comfortable chair and lamp, a small desk for writing in a journal, or a spot for playing music. Honor the sacred directions of north, south, east, west, above, and below by placing sacred objects facing those directions. Hang a wind chime outside the window. Set up a cassette player for listening to music and inspirational tapes that help you turn your attention inward.

A screen, a scroll, and a simple altar in the corner of a room create a place of solitude.

REMODELING OR BUILDING A NEW PLACE OF SOLITUDE

When remodeling or building, consider the following ways of creating a place of solitude. Observe the qualities of the place you are going to remodel or design—shape and proportion; connection to adjacent rooms; size and placement of windows; qualities of light; and other features.

Begin the design of a remodeled place of solitude or a new one by imagining meditating, reading, doing yoga, or listening to music in this room. Envision the furnishings and other elements that will best support your vision of solitude. Think of ways you might alter the existing room or shape the new one to support soulful solitude.

Buy or make a wooden bookshelf for honoring books that you have found which contain special insight and wisdom for you. Create subdued lighting with wall sconces on dimmers and candles. Cover the windows with fabric that transforms the sunlight into a luminous glow. Hang framed stained glass in the window(s). Soften the walls with tapestries or fabric. Hang fabric from the ceiling to create a billowing form. Paint the walls and ceiling with colors that allow your mind and body to settle into a meditative state. Provide for active solitude with wall-to-wall carpeting, mats, or other equipment for yoga and/or exercise.

My ideal place of solitude is a circle twelve feet in diameter. On the east, west, north, and south are niches that hold sacred objects. Below each niche are built-in cabinets that hold sacred and inspirational books. To the southeast, southwest, northwest, and northeast are windows that open to the view or are covered with removable shoji. The floor is covered with tatami mats. Low cushions around the room provide seating.

Doorways, Passageways, and Windows

"A DOOR IS DOUBTLESS THE MOST SIGNIFICANT COMPO-
NENT OF A HOUSE. IT IS OPENED AND CLOSED; IT IS
WHERE WE KNOCK; AND IT IS THE DOOR THAT IS LOCKED.
IT IS THE THRESHOLD AND THE LIMIT. WHEN WE PASS
IN THROUGH OR OUT IT, WE ENTER A SPACE WHERE DIF-
FERENT CONDITIONS PREVAIL, A DIFFERENT STATE OF
CONSCIOUSNESS, BECAUSE IT LEADS TO DIFFERENT PEO-
PLE, A DIFFERENT ATMOSPHERE."

Algernon Blackwood

Transition is a key factor in spiritual experience. The movement from
one state of consciousness to another allows us to touch the otherwise
unmoving depths of the soul. In our homes, our experience of soul
changes as we move through the different rooms. The restfulness of
the bedroom gives way to revitalization in the bathroom, nourishment in the kitchen, unity in the gathering room, and other qualities
of dwelling. The changing light and weather of the days and seasons
that flows through the windows influences our moods and percep-
tions. These transitions in soul experience are given architectural
form by doorways, passageways, and windows.

Inner transformation is personified by Janus, the Roman god of
doors and passageways. Janus is shown with two faces representing

the past and the future. The two faces are often depicted as an old man and a young one. Sometimes one face is female and the other male. The true face of Janus is the invisible face between the past and the future that looks at the elusive present moment. In this regard, Janus was called Master of the Triple Time (past, present, and future), a designation also given to the Indian god Shiva, the dissolver and regenerator of all things. Above all else, Janus is the Lord of Eternity because the Master of Time is not dependent on time.

Janus holds two keys that open and close the gates of time in nature, the winter and summer solstices, the two extreme points of the sun's annual cycle. Being the Master of Time, Janus is the janitor who unlocks and locks this cycle. The month that follows the winter solstice, January, was given his name. The two keys of Janus also represent initiation into spiritual experience. One key is silver, unlocking the knowledge of the earth and the ancestors. The other key is gold, disclosing the wisdom of heaven and the gods.

The doorways over which Janus presides are symbols of hope and opportunity. They provide breaks in the dense material of walls and offer openings to new experience. Each element of a doorway conveys this theme. The threshold marks the boundary of transition, the line that must be crossed to enter new realms of experience. In Europe, such moments of passage were assisted by decorating a threshold with the carving of a pentacle, a five-pointed star signifying harmony and health. In the Balkans, the pentacle was carved into the crossbeam over the door. In a traditional Japanese ritual, salt was sprinkled on the threshold to keep away ghosts.

Frescoed panels adorn the twin pillars of an entry designed by the architect Julia Morgan.

A niche on the crossbeam of an Indian home depicts the figures of Lakshmi (goddess of wealth), a lingam and yoni (symbol of the union of Shiva, the god of transformation, and Shakti, the creative life force), and Nandi, Shiva's mount.

Opposite **A doorway with an arched top by Lawlor/ Weller Design Group softens the passage from one room to another.**

Above and right **Entry gates mark the transition from the public realm to the private, providing a space for turning inward and arriving home.**

Framing either side of the door opening are the twin pillars or doorjambs, representing the guardians of the doorway that must be transcended to reach the security and replenishment within. The twin pillars are unified by the overhead crossbeam. Jews traditionally attach to the doorframe a mezuzah, a small cylinder that contains a written blessing of well-being for those who enter the house.

The door panel hides and reveals the qualities of soul that await beyond the doorway. The lock that secures the door panel is a mystery that must be solved before the doorway can be penetrated. The key is the insight that pierces the mystery of the lock, allowing the door to open.

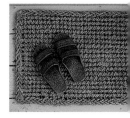

Removing shoes before entering is a simple way to honor the sacredness of a home.

The size and shape of a doorway influences our experience of passing through it. A standard six-foot-eight-inch door seems more intimate than an eight-foot door that towers overhead. An arched doorway gives a feeling of expansion by recalling the vault of the sky. The arch was the emblem of the Roman sky god Jupiter. Arches were often employed at the entries to places used for initiation ceremonies.

Passing through the arch was likened to emerging from a symbolic vulva, leaving behind limited consciousness for a psychological and spiritual rebirth. Square-topped doorways compress consciousness earthward, conveying the experience of groundedness.

PASSAGEWAYS

Hallways and staircases facilitate passage through the rooms of a home. They are threads that bind together the rooms, harmonizing and integrating them. A thread is a symbol of the unseen spiritual power that weaves the fabric of human destiny and binds together the diverse qualities and experiences of life. "On me all things are strung as a row of pearls on a thread," declares Lord Krishna in the Bhagavad Gita. Passageways transform the disparate rooms of a home into a rosary of soul qualities.

A hallway with a finished concrete floor and wood-trimmed doorways serves as a connecting link between the various rooms of a house.

The passage, or path, is the archetypal symbol of spiritual awakening. It embodies the transition from one condition of consciousness to another. The spiritual path is traversed through the rhythmic pulsations of time and is accompanied by the beat of the heart, the cadence of breathing, the meter of sunrise and sunset. These rhythms of soul transformation are honored in a home through the design of its passageways. The regular pattern of a carpet, an orderly arrangement of floorboards, or a grid of ceramic tile supports the measured tread of our footsteps as we travel from the experiences in one room to another over the days and years.

The walls that frame a hallway often enhance this theme. Doorways leading from the hallway to adjacent rooms are sometimes placed at regular intervals. Patterned wallpaper or architectural moldings create a rhythmic scheme. Artwork and photographs can be hung in metered arrangements. Hallway ceilings can reflect these ideas with stenciling or architectural woodwork. Homes without formal hallways create subtler patterns of passage. In open-plan arrangements, for example, furnishings define the path of movement.

Passageways that leave the plane of horizontal movement become staircases. Cultures around the globe use steps or ladders as symbols of the path to spiritual ascension. Jacob's dream in the Old Testament is an example of this idea: "And behold a ladder set up on the earth, and the top of it reached to heaven: and behold the angels of God ascending and descending it." The opening between floors recalls the breakthroughs in understanding or perception that reveal more expanded states of consciousness. Supports and handrails that border

A staircase creates a vertical bridge for the passage of consciousness from one plane of experience to another.

A vaulted atrium adorned with gold leaf establishes a glowing hub that unites the diverse rooms of a home.

A two-story arched window and cathedral ceiling by Lawlor/Weller Design Group integrates the outdoors with a stairway and its adjoining rooms.

Climbing from one stage of experience to another is honored by this ladder stair.

A stair runner employs cows, symbols of the Mother Goddess, and fertile vegetation as a design motif.

Rich golds and greens and stenciling of a vegetal design transform a simple stair into a work of art.

the staircase signify the dark and light, right and wrong, and other pairs of opposites that border the movement toward new realization. Treads unify the pairs of opposites. They support the insights that further each step through the different levels of awakening. Risers separate the treads, lifting or lowering the mind and body toward new stages of experience.

Together, the elements of a staircase create a vertical bridge that symbolically rises through the realms of consciousness, uniting earthly and heavenly experience. Since the base of the stairs rests firmly on the earth, it implies that the path of human ascent must be made from the world of matter to that of spirit. A ladder of seven steps, which are related to the seven major planets, was used in Mithraic initiation ceremonies. Each step was made of the metal that corresponded to the planet it signified.

The shape of a staircase informs the movement of consciousness. A straight run without a landing urges a direct ascent. Stairs with landings offer places to pause along the way. During the early years of

Above **The soul moves in tight twists down a stair with winders.**

Left **A curved staircase invites the soul to flow smoothly and elegantly upward.**

169

this century, Berkeley architect Bernard Maybeck often designed broad stair landings with built-in seating, allowing the transit between floors to be syncopated by a moment of rest. Here one could read a book, contemplate the view through an adjacent window, or converse with a family member or friend. Curved or spiral staircases coil around the central axis of ascent, implying a meandering journey. Winding stairs extend the time spent at each stage of experience savoring the journey to the goal.

WINDOWS

Windows are the eyes of a home. The continuously changing qualities of light that mark the time of day and season of the year connect the rhythms of dwelling to the cycles of nature. Sunlight urges activity; darkness encourages rest. Summer enlivens expansiveness; winter

The opening of dense matter to enliven a home with sunlight and air is celebrated in every detail of this window in Paris.

An arched window softens light views with a graceful curve.

**Harsh sunlight is softened and given
texture by rattan shades.**

invites interior coziness. A window revealing a rainy day can make a home a sleepy place; a window onto a sunny morning can fill it with hopeful possibilities.

Views expand interior spaces and allow them to mingle with the surroundings. The windows that open a kitchen to snowcapped peaks in the Rocky Mountains create a very different atmosphere than windows that look at the brick wall of a city apartment building. Changing views of colors, people, plants, animals, automobiles, and clouds all affect a home's internal environment.

The size, shape, and placement of windows determines the degree to which outside influences are blended with living spaces. Obviously, larger windows create more overlap between interior and exterior. The design and location of a window, however, establishes the qualities of experience and the areas of the surroundings that are invited into a home. A tall, narrow window selects a vertical slice of the environment that stretches from earth to sky. A long, horizontal opening creates an expansive slot that embraces the panorama.

In a bedroom, a circular window provides a view of the heavens, and a row of rectangular windows opens to the earth.

**Stencils of the words
Beauty, Trust, and Harmony
decorate a window next
to a family dining table.**

Placing this type of window low in a wall draws the qualities of earth inside; placed high in a wall, it brings in the sky. An arched window frames the view in a softer way than a rectangular one. Corner windows break open the boundaries of a room, giving a feeling of expansion. Skylights mask out the earth, opening a room only to the dynamic expanse of the sky. Bay windows reach into the surroundings, allowing a room to catch more light and air.

ARRANGING DOORWAYS, PASSAGEWAYS, AND WINDOWS

Use the doorways within your home to honor the transitions from one quality of soul to another as expressed by each room. Honor the transition from the sleep-dream-lovemaking of the bedroom to the purification and renewal of the bathroom, for example, by treating the elements of the doorway with watery design motifs. Paint the door and frame with watery colors and designs. Hang a picture or paint stenciled designs of water over the doorway. Do this with each doorway in your home, acknowledging the specific realm of the soul you enter as you pass into each room. Honor the passage into the kitchen by hanging a picture or stenciled designs of the interaction of fire, water, and earth or fruit and vegetables over and around the doorway.

Honor arrival at and departure from your home in the following ways. Outside the front door, place a welcome mat made of cocoa fibers, jute, or other natural material. On either side of the door, place statues or other objects that represent the primal opposites within creation, such as sun and moon, heaven and earth, male and female. These can be two-dimensional images painted or hung in frames. Hang cloth banners with colorful designs beside the door. Over the door, use images or objects that express the unity of these opposite forces. Install a door knocker designed with the face of a lion or other animal. Hang wreaths and/or swags of dried flowers on the door and change them with the season. Placing a bench or benches near the door creates an inviting feeling.

Inside the front door, put racks and hooks for coats and hats and baskets for gloves and scarves. Find an umbrella stand and place it by the door. Provide well-designed shoe racks and a bench for removing shoes. Hang pictures of Janus, seasonal changes, or other images of transition on the walls of the entry. Place a framed poem or inspirational quote that deals with arrival on a small table. On hot summer days, float a few flowers in a water-filled bowl by the entry. In winter, put out an oil lamp or a cluster of candles.

If you have hallways, enhance the experience of moving through them by hanging pictures of a similar subject at regular intervals along the walls. If the hallway is wide enough, create events along the hallway with a small table or niche for holding flowers or beautiful objects.

Treat stairways in a similar manner to hallways. If the landing is large enough, put a well-lit bookshelf there so you can select a book to read on your way to bed. On the walls of the landing or at the top of the stairs, hang a picture that draws you to look at it. Weave ribbons or garlands of silk flowers through the balustrade.

Treat windows in a similar manner to doorways. Honor the ways in which the forces of nature outside mingle with the qualities of soul specific to each room. In the bedroom, for example, designs of the moon, stars, and sunrise could adorn the window frame and the adjacent walls. The kitchen windows might use the motifs of sun, rain, and food-bearing plants. Use window treatments that are appropriate to the qualities of light that illuminate the characteristics of soul in each room. Heavy drapes could be used to create a quieter light in the bedroom. Filmy curtains would provide more brilliant illumination in the kitchen. Shutters allow gradations of light to enliven a room. Untreated windows connect a room to the changing radiance of the sun throughout the day and the seasons. Windowsills can be used as luminous altars where seashells, objects of colored glass, and other articles can reflect the sun's radiance.

REMODELING OR BUILDING NEW DOORWAYS, PASSAGEWAYS, AND WINDOWS

When remodeling or building, consider the following ways of creating soulful doorways, passageways, and windows. If you are remodeling, observe the qualities of your present doorways, passageways, and windows—shape and proportion; connection to adjacent rooms; size and placement of windows; qualities of light; and other features.

Begin the design of a remodeled entry or a new one by imagining arriving at your home. Envision the approach, door panel, and door surround. Think of the arrivals and departures that will take place here on different occasions—daily comings and goings throughout the seasons, the arrival of mail and packages, the visits of friends and family. Walk through the steps of greeting people to your home—arrival, opening the door, removing coats and hats, and/or putting down packages. Think of ways you might alter the existing entry or shape the new one to support soulful arrival and departure. Use a door panel made of oak or mahogany and make it as thick as possible, or paint the front door with colors and designs that are inviting to soul. Install a solid-brass doorknob that makes entering and leaving your home a special experience.

Remodel or design new interior doorways by imagining walking from one room to another. Think of the materials, shapes, and colors that you associate with soulful movement. Wood-panel doors of oak or mahogany offer grainy texture. Painted flush doors have a quiet simplicity. Think of the forms of door surrounds you could use to honor the activity that takes place within each room—a soft arch for the bedroom, a triangle (the symbol of fire) over the door to the kitchen, a wavy molding over the doorway to the bathroom.

Use a similar approach with passageways. Imagine how moving through your home can enhance soulful experience. A rhythmic succession of pilasters, arches, or wall niches enriches movement from one place to another. Install a floor pattern of inlaid wood, ceramic tile, stone, or patterned carpet. Imagine moving from one floor to another. Think of the shape of a stairway that best supports soulful ascension—straight, switchback, L-shaped, U-shaped, curved, or spiral. Think of the shape, materials, and style of the treads, risers, and handrail. Install a wooden handrail that fits the size and shape of your hand and feels good to the touch. Put a carpet runner up the staircase.

Remodel windows, or design new ones, by imagining how they will illuminate the characteristics of soul in each room. Envision the direction the windows will face and the time of day that each room is usually used. Think of the qualities of sunlight that will best illuminate each room—quiet morning light for breakfast, brightness in the home office, or intimate sunset glow for the gathering room. Design the size and shape of the windows by imagining the amount of light that will best illuminate the soulfulness of each room—small cozy windows in the bedroom, a medium glow in the bathroom, and large windows in the gathering room. Take the potential view from each room into account and use the window to artfully frame the section of the view you want. In this case, bigger is not always better; soulfulness is enhanced by the interplay of the boundaries of the wall with the unboundedness of the window's view. At stairways, install a window at the landing or top of the stairs. This will draw your eye upward toward the light and view.

A soulful alternative to an electric doorbell.

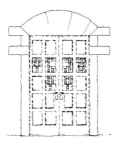

13

Gardens

A HOME FOR THE SOUL WOULD NOT BE COMPLETE WITH-
OUT SOME TYPE OF GARDEN. THE SPIRIT CANNOT DWELL
IN WHOLENESS UNLESS IT IS TOUCHED BY THE HARMONY
AND BEAUTY OF PLANTS, SOIL, AND THE NATURAL PRO-
CESSES OF GROWTH. EVEN A FEW POTTED PLANTS OR A
VASE OF FLOWERS IN AN APARTMENT CAN CONNECT US
WITH THE RENEWING POWERS OF A GARDEN. "THE GREAT-
EST DELIGHT WHICH THE WOODS AND FIELDS MINISTER
IS THE SUGGESTION OF AN OCCULT RELATION BETWEEN
MAN AND VEGETABLE. I AM NOT ALONE AND UNAC-
KNOWLEDGED. THEY NOD TO ME AND I TO THEM," WROTE
EMERSON. IN A GARDEN THE SOUL FINDS HARMONY
BETWEEN THE OPPOSING FORCES OF LIFE. SUN AND
WATER, EARTH AND AIR, MINERAL AND VEGETABLE, MALE
AND FEMALE, AND OTHER FORCES OF DUALITY WORK
TOGETHER IN ECOLOGIES OF HEALTH AND VITALITY.
DYING LEAVES AND FLOWERS BECOME THE FERTILE SOIL
OF NEW LIFE.

Gardens are symbols of paradise—the primordial state of innocence, peace, and unity. Divine forces create and tend the garden, generating an infinitely diverse web of existence. The mythic image of paradise often has a Tree of Eternal Life growing at the center as a sign of the source and goal of spiritual understanding. A spring at the base of the tree feeds four rivers that flow to the four directions, dividing the garden into four quadrants. When surrounded by walls or hedges, gardens represent virginity and the feminine principle of protective nurturing.

Expulsion from the garden, or forgetting its importance in human dwelling, indicates a fall from a unified, integrated state of consciousness into one of duality and conflict. Adam and Eve were banished from Eden after eating from the tree whose fruit contained the duality of good and evil. Leaving the garden, we enter a realm of darkness, chaos, and hardship; a land of "thistles and thorns" where nourishment is gained only by hard work and the sweat of one's brow. Reentering the garden signifies a return to our true nature, a life in harmony with growth and transformation.

For the Greeks, the god Pan personified the integration of mind and body found in gardens. The upper half of Pan's body is human, the lower half is animal. In one myth, Pan chased the nymph Syrinx to the shore of the River Ladon. Trapped, with no means of escape, Syrinx hoped to hide from Pan and begged the gods to transform her into a cluster of reeds. Pan was not fooled by this disguise. He cut the reeds and combined their different lengths to make his musical pipes. In this way, Pan symbolizes the integration of earthy lustiness with the music of the cosmic melodies. Under the influence of Pan, the fleeting nature of the mind is grounded in the reeds and soil, harmonizing spirit and matter. Another myth describes the mournful cry that arose from the rocks, plants, and animals when they heard that Pan had died, that mind and body had been separated.

PLANTS

From the perspective of the soul, trees are the most dominant plants in the garden. Their roots, trunk, and spreading branches span the full spectrum of the consciousness. Rooted in the earth, trees reach toward the heavens. Plato said that "[a human being] is like a celestial plant . . . an inverted tree, of which the roots [mental functions] stretch towards the heavens and the branches [bodily functions] stretch towards the earth." The roots represent the universal principles that support and nourish the diverse branches, leaves, flowers, and fruit. The sap recalls the powers of the soul that sustain the visible manifestation of the tree of life. Trees also convey immortality. Evergreens display the unchanging depths of the soul, while deciduous trees show the eternal spirit that survives the death and rebirth of the seasons. In mythic terms, a tree is seen as the world axis, the central organizing principle about which the universe rotates.

Flowers are symbols of freshness and vitality. They herald the youthful joy of spring, the celebration of victory over death in winter. Flowers are also emblems of impermanence. "The flowers sprout and grow, and glow. From within you the stalks spring freely. . . . Like a flower in the summertime, so does our heart take refreshment and bloom. Our body is like a flower that blossoms and quickly withers," wrote an Aztec poet. Buds connote hope and possibility. Opening outward from the center, they make manifest the radiance of consciousness and the expansion of the heart. The cuplike shape of flowers conveys receptivity. Buddha, the embodiment of awakened consciousness and compassion, is depicted as sitting on a lotus flower. Blue flowers signify the unattainable. Red petals recall the dawn, the rising sun, passion, and the Mother Goddess. White flowers indicate purity. Scented flowers were thought to provide protection from negative influences.

A wooden porch becomes living architecture by training morning glories to cover this east-facing entry.

Rose

Roses are rich with symbolism. "In the form then of a pure rose the holy host was shown to me," wrote Dante in his *Paradiso*. Roses simultaneously embody the passion of human life and the perfection of the divine, time and timelessness, mortality and immortality, maidenhood and motherhood. As the flower of Christ, the rose is linked with the heart center of spiritual love. As the flower of Venus, it is connected with the carnal love of romantic seduction and wine. Roses in the form of rosettes are often used as motifs in architecture and interior design. A four-petaled pattern recalls the four directions and the

cross. Five petals indicate the microcosm of human life; six petals, the universal macrocosm.

Lotus

In the East, lotus flowers carry the same meaning as roses. The lotus depicts the seven circles of consciousness, or chakras, in the body that are awakened in the growth of spiritual experience. Joseph Campbell describes the significance of the lotus in *The Mythic Image:* "The lotus, then, symbolizes both the sun and the heart as the sun of the body, both moved by the same indwelling Self. And accordingly, the lotus open to the sun symbolizes the fully flowered knowledge of this mirrored truth."

Lily

Lilies are sacred to both the goddesses of virginity and fertility, signifying purity and new life.

Orchids

Orchids convey luxury and splendor; the Chinese use orchids to represent the refinement and beauty of perfection in human life.

Iris

The iris is hope and the power of light.

Peony

In China, the peony is a masculine flower representing prosperity and radiant illumination; it was designated the flower of the royal family.

Poppy

The poppy is sacred to the lunar deities, signifying fertility and sleep.

Pansy

Pansy, from the French *pensée,* literally means "thought," and the pansy is therefore a symbol of meditation and remembrance.

Hyacinth

The hyacinth represents spiritual aspiration and resurrection.

A stone
pavilion in
a Roman
garden
offers
shelter
from the
sweltering
sun while
opening to
cooling
breezes.

ROCKS

Rocks embody the immovable and unchanging. They are the masculine force in the otherwise feminine realm of flowers and leafy plants. In numerous cultures, gods were said to be born as rocks. Mithras, the Persian god of light, emerged from a rock. In Japan and China, the shape of a rock expresses the particular qualities of spirit dwelling within it. In Ireland and India, stones are thought to hold spiritual power and transmit life force and sometimes bring fertility to women who are unable to conceive.

Rocks can take many forms in a garden. Rough stones or boulders can become focal points or accents to greenery. An area of pebbles or sand such as those found in Japanese rock gardens can create a field of

grainy texture. In Zen gardens, boulders set within sand raked in undulating patterns are often used to depict mountainous crags surrounded by a turbulent ocean. Stepping-stones and paving offer firm supports for traversing soft grasses or pebbles. A shaded stone bench offers a setting of cool repose in summer. Stone walls can define a firm boundary for an inner garden of undefinable complexity. Stone retaining walls can be used to create terraced gardens that recall the ascending steps of spiritual awakening.

Architecture comes alive by weaving plants into an entry gate.

Alternating the heights of pickets adds liveliness to a fence.

**Rocks establish the immutable qualities
of soul in a garden. A garden pool creates a
place of reflection and contemplation.
Fish signify the vital powers of life that arise
from the depths of the soul.**

WATER

Water springing from crevices between rocks is a sign of the spirit breaking forth into the world. In a garden, water spawns, sustains, kills, and replenishes life. Water awakens fertility in the soil and urges the sprouting of seeds. Drawn in through the roots, it flows to the trunks, stems, leaves, and flowers, preserving the life of plants and trees. The growth cycle dies when water becomes frost and snow. As spring rain, water softens the frozen ground in preparation for rebirth.

In many cultures, water is said to be the dwelling place of spirits and nymphs—beings that personify the vital forces contained in water. They signify specific qualities of consciousness arising from the depths of the soul. Vedic mythology describes water spirits called *apsaras*, who descend from heaven to catch the attention of and delight ascetics. One tale relates the love that King Puruavas shared with a water nymph named Urvashi. Mermaids offer a well-known image of water spirits. Half woman and half fish, a mermaid is a watery version of Pan. They display a fluid form of mind-body integration that dissolves the boundary between conscious and unconscious experience.

Beyond its power to generate growth, water can express numerous qualities of the soul. In fountains, water signifies the source of vitality, the spring of immortality. Placed at the center of a courtyard or garden, a fountain recalls the world navel and hub of the cosmos. Jets of water springing from the mouths of sculptures symbolize the awakening powers of knowledge and speech. Ponds and pools create settings of visual and mental reflection. Created in low-lying places or basins, ponds and pools signify the receptive mind that can collect wisdom.

BIRDS

Birds add to the soulful experience in a garden. Birds portray the soaring nature of the spirit, movement toward expanded states of awareness, and the power to communicate with the divine. They are

Garden and home overlap on a covered porch.

A miniature sacred garden is created by burning incense before a bonsai.

often used as emblems of the soul when it leaves the body at death.

The Greek tale of Icarus describes a man who fashioned wings from feathers and wax, flew too close to the sun, and when the wax melted, plunged into the sea. The story warns that grandiose aspirations which ignore the laws of nature lead to disaster. A bird holding a snake depicts the victory of spiritual awakening over our base instincts. The Upanishads use the image of two birds to symbolize the relationship between the active surface of the mind and its silent depths; one bird busily eats the fruit of a tree while the other one quietly watches. Power is depicted by eagles, hawks, and falcons; peace, by doves and swans; wisdom, by owls, ravens, and pelicans.

A winter garden can be created by hanging dried flowers on a wall and placing living plants near a window.

Arranging a Soulful Garden

It would take an entire book to describe the creation of a soulful garden, but here are a few suggestions. Inside your house or apartment, create mini-gardens with plants, water, and rocks.

By a window, place a bowl of water or a small fountain and surround it with houseplants and an assortment of stones. If you have enough space, make this small garden large enough to contain a bench. If you have sufficient light, use ficus and other large indoor plants as the "trees" in your garden. Use smaller plants to create the "garden." If you want to go all the way, complete the setting with a beautiful birdcage and birds.

If space is limited, "force" the bulbs of paper-whites, tulips, daffodils, hyacinths, or crocuses in bowls filled with gravel or small stones. Light an aroma candle that spreads the fragrance of fresh flowers. Place wreaths of dried flowers on tables, walls, and doors. Make the wall of a room a garden wall by hanging prints of flowering plants, birds, or paradise gardens. Place a bird feeder outside your window.

Remodeling or Building a New Garden

When remodeling or building, consider the following ways of creating a soulful garden. Observe the land you are going to cultivate—size and shape of lot, slope, existing plants and trees, available sunlight, climate, and other features.

Begin the design of the garden by imagining how the outdoor areas can nourish the qualities of soul expressed in the different rooms of the house. Design the garden so that the areas next to each room extend the soulful qualities of that room into the environment by choosing plants, shrubs, trees, colors, fountains, and other elements that connect indoor activities with the out-of-doors. Imagine being in the garden at different times of the day and year. Visualize the various activities you will engage in there—sitting, reading, barbecuing, dining. Think of how you might use paths, gateways, benches, pergolas, trellises, walls, fences, and other elements to support these activities.

Use materials that you find soulful, such as brick or bluestone for paths, fieldstone for walls, cedar for trellises. Mix flowers and vegetables to make an edible garden. Use plants that are native to your microclimate. Install a sundial to connect the location of your garden to its place on the earth and relationship to the sun. Install birdhouses and bird feeders.

PART TWO

Personal Images of the Soul

14

Mandala of the Soul

A mandala is a symbolic diagram that describes fundamental images and patterns of existence. It is a snapshot of our true nature, a microcosm of the soul's totality. The Mandala of the Soul described below can be used as a tool for discovering and exploring images that can assist you in creating a home for the soul.

Mandala is a Sanskrit word meaning "circle," and mandalas depict the circle of the soul, showing the full spectrum of qualities and cycles through which living proceeds. A mandala of the day would show the images and cycles of sunrise, morning, noon, afternoon. A mandala of the year would revolve around the four seasons. Mandalas that describe the forces that uphold the creation and evolution of the universe are used to design the floor plans of Indian temples. Temples constructed on these sacred diagrams are seen as embodiments of all the qualities of energy and intelligence that structure world order.

Carl Jung saw mandalas as depictions of innate archetypes, the images and patterns of the soul that guide our thoughts and actions. In this sense, mandalas reveal images of our spiritual essence, the seed forms that contain the tree of our existence. These seed forms show the threads of soul transformation, the fibers of the psyche, that can be addressed to enliven the whole person.

THE ARK OF SOUL

In his studies of medieval alchemy, Jung found that separation is a fundamental process of soul work. An alchemical operation called *separatio* was regarded as essential in transforming common materials into gold. In psychological terms, Jung saw *separatio* as the identifying of the different soul materials that needed attention. When seen as a unified mass, these materials were too condensed and their individual needs could not be cared for. When our bodies, for example, have aches and pains, we don't massage the whole body at once; we tend to those muscles and organs that are fatigued, stimulating the flow of blood to the whole system. By differentiating the threads of the soul's fabric, we can identify those parts of ourselves that need care and those that can be fostered to enrich our lives.

The Mandala of the Soul identifies the compartments within the psyche that correspond to the rooms found in almost every dwelling place. It is a psychological cabinet, a collection of cubbyholes that contain personally significant images of soul. By using the mandala to identify those parts of the soul that need care, we can use our homes as settings to revitalize the wholeness of our lives.

Sacred cabinets of this sort have long been used to identify and display objects of spiritual power. The Ark of the Covenant and the Christian tabernacle are two examples of religious cabinets in this tradition. In homes, china cabinets often take on this function. In her book *Ordinarily Sacred*, Lynda Sexson describes a china cabinet that an old man filled with possessions of his wife, who had died. These images, containing the soul activity of the old man's lifetime companion, were given a place of honor allowing him to deepen the communion of their love even though they were apart.

Cabinets such as these establish arks of sacredness. Arks embody the notion of arcane teachings, secret knowledge that is locked away as if in a chest. Arks hold obscure wisdom to which outsiders have no access. They are houses of mystery, symbols of the womb from which all life miraculously springs forth. The ark of a crescent moon is an

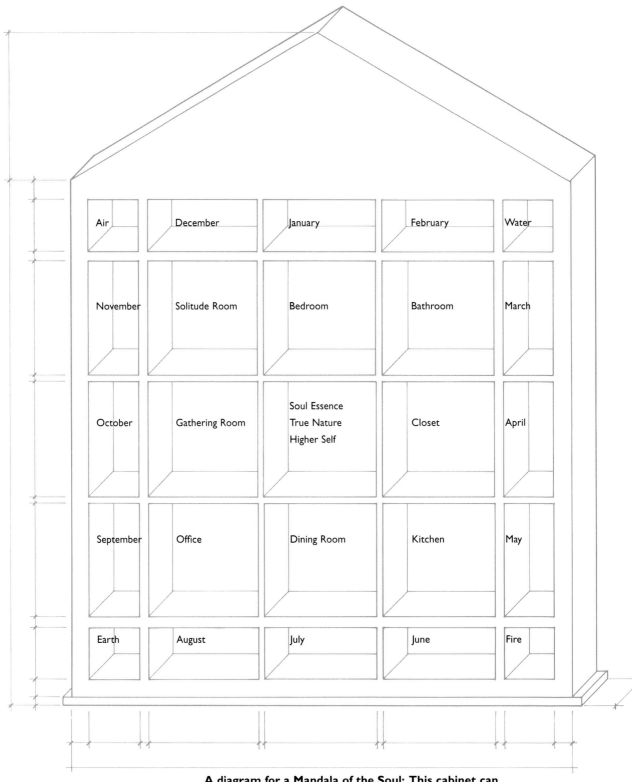

Air · December · January · February · Water

November · Solitude Room · Bedroom · Bathroom · March

October · Gathering Room · Soul Essence True Nature Higher Self · Closet · April

September · Office · Dining Room · Kitchen · May

Earth · August · July · June · Fire

A diagram for a Mandala of the Soul: This cabinet can provide a structure for discovering the forms, colors, and textures of your home for the soul.

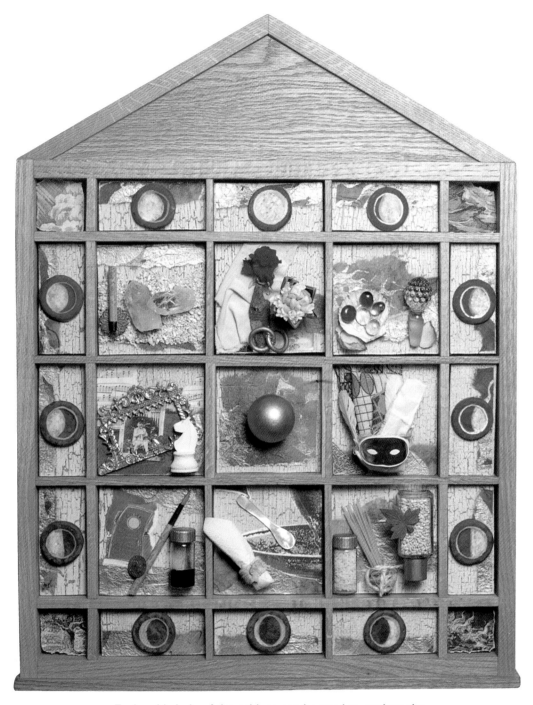

**Each cubbyhole of the cabinet can be used to explore the
images that embody a different aspect of your personality.**

ancient symbol of the ship of destiny floating through the boundless deep of the sky. Riding the waves of flooding waters, arks, such as Noah's, carry the seeds of life. The Ark of the Covenant represents the Divine Presence, the abode of God. It was said to be made of indestructible wood and covered with gold.

THREE CIRCLES OF EXPERIENCE

At the center of the mandala cabinet is your spiritual essence. Encircling your spiritual essence is the ring of thoughts and actions within your mind and body. Surrounding your mind and body is the circle of climatic and seasonal change.

In relation to the mandala, your core spiritual essence is what you consider to be the foundation of your life, the source of your thoughts, words, and actions. This essence is the animator of your body and the world. Some might call it God. Others would say it is the Self, Pure Consciousness, or True Nature. A scientist might call it energy or the quantum field.

Bounding your core spiritual essence are the thoughts and actions of dwelling. Whether you live in a one-room apartment or a multi-room mansion, your home has eight basic activity areas: bedroom, bathroom, dressing room, kitchen, dining room, home office, gathering room, and solitude room. These activity areas may overlap or share a common space—the dining room may be in the kitchen, or the dressing room might be within the bedroom and the bedroom in the living room—but these are the essential building blocks of a home. Each of these eight "rooms" expresses a different thread of your soul. Dreams that emanate from the soul are expressed in the bedroom. The soul's desire to care for the body is made tangible in the bathroom. Self-image is manifested in the dressing room. Family relates to the nourishment of the kitchen; wealth to the abundance of dining; career and commerce to the home office; friendship to gathering; and knowledge to solitude.

Encircling the activities of inhabiting are the environmental influences of sunlight (fire), rain (water), wind (air), landforms, plants, and animals (earth). The cycles of day and night and the round of the four seasons continuously change and renew the life of a home.

Linking the soul to the three layers of shelter described by the mandala—spiritual essence, body/mind inhabiting, and environment—are the images that we associate with the activities of living. Soul might be linked to the kitchen, for example, by an image of bread in the oven or soup simmering on the stove. By using the Mandala of the Soul to identify the images that link your heart and mind to the rooms that shelter, you can deepen soulful connections to your present home. These images can in turn provide a fertile storehouse of images for selecting colors, design forms, materials, and furnishings that can be used to remodel or build a home for the soul.

Spiritual essence

The rooms of the house

The natural surroundings of the house

PERSONAL SYMBOLS OF SOUL

The mandala deepens the meaning and significance of dwelling by offering a means of discovering symbols of the soul that are personal to you. These symbols describe the leading characters in the story of your life. They are key figures in your personal mythology. The images that you associate with the various cubbies of the mandala connect the particulars of your life with the deep movements of soul, those that also shape the eternal, mythic themes of creation. Personal symbols that make such connections do not have to be grandiose. The form and color of a child's toy or a favorite chair, for example, can connect the details of living to the deep currents of the psyche. Symbols that embody the common, yet timeless, actions of sleeping, lovemaking, cooking, or eating allow the momentary events of the day to touch eternal themes of living.

The themes of your personal story of dwelling in the world can be discovered in the mandala through the use of various types of symbols. Mythic gods, common objects, geometric shapes, plants, animals, people, colors, and qualities of light are among the symbolic forms that can be used. The purpose of applying symbolic images to the "rooms" of the mandala is not to intellectually figure out who you are. The purpose is to feel the shapes of soul movement within you. The intent is to find the images that allow you to stand on the borderline where the unfathomable mystery of your soul nature meets the thoughts and actions that create your life. The mandala is not a puzzle to be solved; it is a pattern of living to be explored.

You can make a mandala in several ways: by creating a three-dimensional mandala of wood (or ordering one ready-made), by drawing a mandala structure on a large piece of paper on a table, or by creating the mandala on a rug using yarn to demarcate the "rooms."

Each member of your household can create his or her own Mandala of the Soul. By honoring the images of dwelling that each persona holds dear, meaningful connections between family members can be shared and deepened. Don't edit, criticize, smirk at, make

Suzanne Thomas Lawlor made these collages for a table
mandala (shown on page 203). They depict her enthusiasm
for the goddess as celebrated in Vedic, Christian, and Native
American traditions and reflect her love of meditation,
family, friends, and nature.

Left **Yarn was stretched in a grid pattern on a rug and secured with straight pins to make this family mandala. Full-scale objects were then used to create the images in the different squares.**

fun of, or denigrate anyone's images. This is an opportunity for each person to share intimate thoughts and know one another's needs and dreams. Look at the images and feel the common themes; also, acknowledge and honor the rich diversity of soul among you.

Create a household mandala by working together and putting images developed by the group in their appropriate "rooms" of the diagram.

MAKING A MANDALA OF THE SOUL

You can make a cabinet to house objects that symbolize the qualities of soul you associate with different rooms. Use the plan provided on page 216. In each of the boxes mentioned below, place pictures and/or objects that depict the qualities of soul within you that relate to the different squares of the mandala. Give your imagination free rein; express who you are. If you get stuck on a particular square, sit quietly, settle into yourself, think the name of the room (e.g., kitchen) or month (e.g., May), and see what images arise. Take your time and allow the images to rise spontaneously into your awareness. Let this be an opportunity to listen and respond to the qualities of nourishment your soul desires.

You can also draw the mandala on a large piece of butcher paper. Paste images from magazines or draw your own within the squares of the grid. To give the drawing a three-dimensional quality, use small items to represent how each room reflects your heart and mind.

If you would like to use full-scale objects, such as tea pots, hats, books, or other items as emblems of the soul, make a large mandala on the floor. Form the gird by stretching yarn or twine across a carpet. Search the various rooms of your home for objects and mementos that depict how your soul is expressed in physical form.

Right **This cabinet mandala was made of oak following the plans on page 216. It was then laid flat on a table and the objects and collage fragments were glued down with Elmer's glue. Picture frame wire was attached to the back and the cabinet was hung on a wall.**

Below **Suzanne Lawlor's table mandala was drawn on a large piece of illustration board. Collage images and small objects were attached with rubber cement and Elmer's glue so the board could be hung on the wall.**

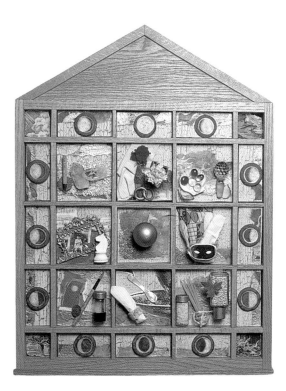

1 Central Square: Soul Essence

Bring your attention to the central "room" of the mandala. Imagine the symbol(s) that embodies your spiritual essence. It may be a religious figure or teacher, such as Christ, Buddha, Mary, or Kuan-yin. The geometric shape of a Star of David, cross, or yin-yang circle may fulfill the purpose. A bear, eagle, or other animal form might be appropriate. Is there a flower, tree, or plant that describes the core of your being? What color(s) would you paint this central square? Which qualities of light reflect the mood? Is there a common object such as an egg or a wedding ring that somehow captures your spiritual essence?

2 Upper Center: Bedroom

Above the central square is a rectangle entitled
Bedroom. Within this box, place the images of
sleeping, dreaming, and lovemaking that connect
universal soul to personal soul. What images come to
mind that depict the mystery and peace of sleep?
Remember the dream images that have meaning for
you. Are there dream people, places, objects,
events, or feelings that have had an impact on you?
Picture the symbols that describe the longing,
sensuality, and union of lovemaking.

3 Upper Right: Bathroom

In the square entitled Bathroom, place the symbol(s) that depicts the washing and beautifying of the body. What images convey the idea of caring for the soul through bathing? Do mythic figures, such as Venus rising out of the ocean on a seashell, come to mind? What colors, textures, and fragrances symbolize health and personal care?

4 Center Right: Closet

For Closet, think of the symbols that depict how you want to appear to others. Think of how you dress for the different roles you play: mother or father, businessperson, partygoer, athlete, student. What fabrics and colors do you like to wear? Choose one article of clothing or accessory that embodies who you are, such as a pair of glasses, a hat, or a coat.

5 Bottom Right: Kitchen

For Kitchen, remember your childhood impressions
of cooking and the daily activities of family life.
What did you help your mother prepare: chocolate
chip cookies, cakes, or other food? What images
symbolize the warming qualities of the hearth and
the gathering of family members to create a
nourishing meal?

6 Center Bottom: Dining Room

For Dining, imagine enjoying a feast of all the best that life has to offer. What symbolizes an abundant banquet for you? Envision the circle of a dinner plate and find images or objects that you would put within the circle to depict nourishment. What would you place around the circle of the plate to portray a sense of nourishment and fulfillment?

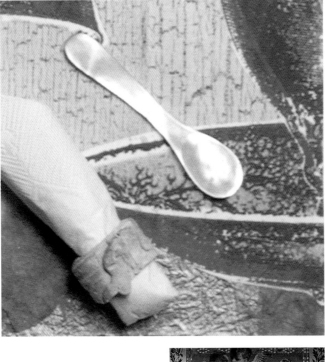

7 Bottom Left: Office

For Office, bring to mind the images that embody the soul of work and the power of money. What portrays the work you would like to be doing? Is there a piece of equipment that represents the talents you want to express? For a writer this might be a pen; for an architect a T square or compass; an attorney might use a scale of justice. What symbols depict your feelings about money? Do you see money as a warrior god or a benevolent, peaceful goddess?

8 Left Center: Gathering Room

In the Gathering Room box, place symbols that convey a sense of benevolence, compassion, and unity among people. What images show how individuals join together to share knowledge, for entertainment, to comfort one another in times of sorrow, and celebrate in times of joy?

9 Upper Left: Solitude Room

For Solitude, settle into a state of silence. What emblems of knowledge are meaningful to you? Is there a particular spiritual tradition, deity, teacher, or book that is a source of inspiration and wisdom? What images portray moments of insight you have had? What pictures and objects depict the ways you enjoy solitude, such as meditating, journal writing, listening to music, exercising?

You have completed the inner ring of your Mandala of the Soul, the images and symbols that structure the sacred home within you. The outer ring of your mandala is made up of the environmental influences that affect your experience of dwelling in the world. As you did with the inner ring of boxes, place pictures and objects that describe your relationship to the climate, landforms, animals, culture, and events that surround you.

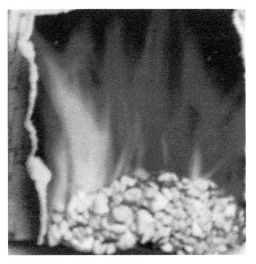

10 Upper Right Corner: Water

Place in this box images that portray the beauty and power of water, such as rain, snow, dewdrops, lakes, rivers, waterfalls, oceans, fountains, springs, baptismal fonts, water lilies, lotuses, and fish.

11 Lower Right Corner: Fire

In the lower right square, place the symbols that express the wonder of life-giving warmth, such as the sun, stars, fireplaces, candles, and stoves.

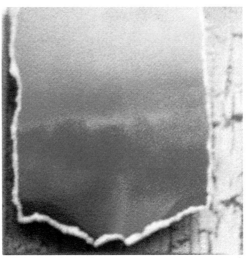

12 Lower Left Corner: Earth

In the lower left-hand corner, put pictures and objects that depict the earth's nourishing abundance, such as flowers, seeds, fruits, vegetables, trees, animals, mountains, valleys, stones, and gems.

13 Upper Left Corner: Air

In the upper left-hand corner, place images and objects that show the inspiration of air, such as clouds, birds in flight, prayer flags in the wind, curtains lifted by a breeze, a flute or wind chime.

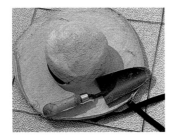

March

14 Outer Border: The Months

In the remaining boxes, place images or objects that express your associations with the seasons and months of the year. Think of the holidays, birthdays, anniversaries, and other events that are important to you. What are the symbols that embody these events? What symbol depicts your birthday or wedding anniversary? Bring to mind the qualities of each month, such as the freshness of May, the hot, lazy days of August, or the brisk, busy feeling of November. If you are interested in astrology, look at your astrological chart and place the various planets in the months that correspond to their house. If your chart indicates that your Moon is in Cancer, put a symbol of the moon in the July box; if Venus is in Libra, place a symbol of beauty in the October box; do this with each of the planets in your horoscope.

April

September

Using the Mandala of the Soul

Images from your Mandala of the Soul can assist you in developing design themes in your house or apartment. The pictures and objects you selected embody specific motifs that can link inner qualities of consciousness to outer architecture and furnishings. Creating a home that expresses the themes depicted in your mandala can establish a harmonious relationship between your soul and your surroundings.

Look at your mandala and notice the colors, shapes, and textures of the images. Use of color can indicate a particular design mood. A predominance of blue, for example, might indicate a design mood of peacefulness, coolness, harmony, and fantasy. If two or more colors stand out in your mandala, the mood of your design theme can reflect a range of feelings and experiences. Below is a chart of colors and the design moods they indicate:

White	*purity, cleanliness, delicacy, refinement, precision*
Black	*power, dignity*
Red	*excitement, activity, romance, warmth*
Orange	*casualness, autumn*
Yellow	*transformation, attracts attention, complexity*
Blue	*peacefulness, coolness, harmony, and fantasy*
Blue-green	*prestige, stylishness*
Green	*stability, food, sophistication*
Brown	*informality, earthiness*
Gray	*creativity, exclusivity, success*

Particular shapes can be used as indicators of your design style. Abstract, geometric shapes, such as squares and triangles, might imply a minimalist approach. Organic forms, such as seashells and leaves, could point toward an earthy or craftsman style. A combination of shapes could indicate an eclectic approach. Notice the shapes that appear in your mandala. Are they angular, rounded, or free-form? Do the images reflect a particular period in history, such as classical Greece, the Victorian era, or a contemporary design trend.

Texture can indicate the materials that nourish your soul. Smoothness may imply the use of materials such as Sheetrock walls, ceramic-tile floors, glass tables, painted cabinets and doors, and polished stone countertops. Roughness might indicate the use of wool carpets, raw-silk fabrics, arrangements of dried flowers, wall-hangings, and tapestries. A fine-grained texture might imply flooring, furniture, doors, and cabinets of hardwood.

A recurring image in your mandala can be used as a primary symbol that informs each element of your design. If trees, for example, crop up again and again, think of what trees mean to you and use that meaning as a guiding idea in your design. If you think of trees as symbols of sturdiness and shelter, choose furnishings, colors, and other elements that convey those feelings—chairs that are solid, a four-poster bed that shelters, candelabra that branch out, or earthy shades of brown and green. If the sun is a recurring theme, reflect the radiance and warmth of sunlight in your home.

Go room by room through the mandala and use the mood(s) of color, style(s) of design, and texture(s) of materials to transform your dwelling place into a home that nourishes your soul.

CREATING A MANDALA OF THE SOUL CABINET

The easiest way to construct a cabinet mandala is to have pieces of oak, maple, cherry, or other hardwood precut to the dimensions listed below. Join the pieces according to the diagram and fasten them together with Elmer's wood glue.

If you wish to purchase a Mandala of the Soul Cabinet ready-made, contact Lawlor/Weller Design Group, PO Box 1272, Fairfield, IA 52556, (515) 472-4561.

Shopping for Wood

No.	Size, in inches (height x width x depth)	Qty
1	$\frac{3}{4}$ x $21\frac{1}{4}$ x $2\frac{7}{8}$	2
2	$19\frac{3}{4}$ x $\frac{3}{4}$ x $2\frac{7}{8}$	2
3	$\frac{3}{8}$ x 22 x 3	1
4	$\frac{3}{8}$ x $19\frac{3}{4}$ x $2\frac{7}{8}$	2
5	$\frac{1}{4}$ x $19\frac{3}{4}$ x $2\frac{7}{8}$	2
6	$2\frac{1}{8}$ x $\frac{3}{8}$ x $2\frac{7}{8}$	4
7	$2\frac{1}{8}$ x $\frac{1}{4}$ x $2\frac{7}{8}$	4
8	$4\frac{3}{4}$ x $3\frac{3}{8}$ x $2\frac{7}{8}$	6
9	$4\frac{3}{4}$ x $\frac{1}{4}$ x $2\frac{7}{8}$	6
10	$5\frac{5}{8}$ x $19\frac{1}{2}$ x $\frac{1}{4}$	1
11	$\frac{3}{8}$ x $12\frac{1}{4}$ x 3	2
12	$26\frac{7}{8}$ x $21\frac{1}{4}$ x $\frac{1}{4}$	1

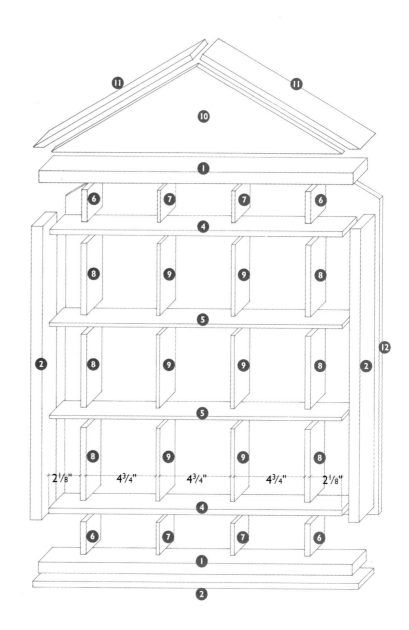

15

Continuous Discovery

A HOME FOR THE SOUL IS NOT A FINAL DESTINATION. IT IS
A PROCESS OF SELF-DISCOVERY THAT DEEPENS OVER TIME.
WE MAY SEEK A DWELLING PLACE WHERE STABILITY AND
CONTENTMENT ARE ATTAINED ONCE AND FOR ALL, BUT THIS
DOES NOT SEEM TO BE THE NATURE OF A SOULFUL LIFE. AS
SOON AS ONE GOAL IS ACHIEVED, A FRESH DESIRE ARISES.
THE PLEASURE OF THE SOUL APPEARS TO BE FOUND IN THE
JOURNEY OF DISCOVERY, THE UNFOLDING REVELATION OF
EXPANDED INSIGHT AND EXPERIENCE.

As you continue living in your present home or move to new ones, I
hope the discussions and images in this book travel with you, encour-
aging you to dwell with spirit and imagination. I hope that the rooms
and furniture that surround you become active participants in a life of
vitality, depth, and meaning, an environment where your spirit can
thrive. Sometimes nothing may seem to happen, but with care and
attention, soulfulness can grow, another chamber of your true nature
can be opened. Sacredness can deepen and life can expand. The
ancient tracks of the spirit's trail can be rediscovered and your soul
can find its way home.

Bibliography

Ayto, John. *Dictionary of Word Origins.* New York: Arcade Publishing, 1990.

Biedermann, Hans. *Dictionary of Symbolism.* New York: Meridian, 1994.

Campbell, Joseph. *The Hero With a Thousand Faces.* Princeton, N.J.: Princeton University Press, 1973.

———. *The Mythic Image.* Princeton, N.J.: Princeton University Press, 1974.

Cooper, J. C. *The Illustrated Encyclopaedia of Traditional Symbols.* London: Thames and Hudson, 1978.

Cousineau, Phil. *Soul: An Archaeology.* New York: HarperCollins Publishers, 1994.

Eliade, Mircea. *The Forge and the Crucible.* Chicago and London: University of Chicago Press, 1978.

Grant, Michael, and John Hazel. *Who's Who in Classical Mythology.* New York: Oxford University Press, 1993.

Guénon, René. *Fundamental Symbols.* Cambridge, England: Quinta Essentia, 1995.

Hamilton, Edith. *Mythology.* New York: Mentor, 1969.

Hillman, James. *Blue Fire.* New York: Harper Perennial, 1991.

———. *Facing the Gods.* Dallas: Spring Publications, 1980.

Lame Deer, John (Fire), and Richard Erdoes. *Lame Deer, Seeker of Visions.* New York: Pocket Books, 1972.

Moore, Thomas. *Care of the Soul.* New York: HarperCollins Publishers, 1992.

Reps, Paul. *Zen Flesh, Zen Bones.* Garden City, N.Y.: Anchor Books, 1961.

Stern, James. *The Complete Grimm's Fairy Tales.* New York: Pantheon Books, 1972.

Tanizaki, Jun'ichiro. *In Praise of Shadows.* New Haven, Conn.: Leete's Island Books, 1977.

Illustration Credits

All drawings are by Anthony
Lawlor. Except as noted below, all
photographs are by Rick
Donhauser.

Allen Donhauser: page 25 right.

Art Grice: page 28.

Anthony Lawlor: pages 2, 21, 27,
34, 35, 36, 47, 56 bottom, 96, 104
bottom, 107, 110, 111, 140, 162,
163 top, 165 top left and bottom,
167 center, 168 left, 170,
171 left, 177, 178, 181, 183, 184,
185, 188 top.

Mark Paul Petrick: pages 39 top,
142, 163.